LIVING IN A
TEST TUBE

To Reyn Stocks a good
Christian lady and educator.
May God bless you
always.

Patry Dee

LIVING IN A
TEST TUBE

A SCIENTIFIC
TO BIBLICAL
PARALLEL

BY L.E. LEE

To order additional copies of this book, contact:
Xlibris Corporation
1-888-795-4274
www.Xlibris.com
Orders@Xlibris.com
116140

TABLE OF CONTENTS

INTRODUCTION

As far back as man can see, and the written record can attest to, there has been a struggle—a war if you will—against the spiritual forces of good and evil. Within the earliest fringes of time according to the sacred scriptures, a war broke out in heaven. **"And there was war in Heaven:"** Rev. 12:7

What do you mean a war in heaven? The event itself does not even sound right! Let alone to have actually taken place. The question of what happened up there immediately comes to the inquiring mind and to the ardent student of the Bible. Who or what in creation would attempt to go against their creator and Maker, God? The test is already in place, and this usurper has failed it. Whatever his test was, he failed it! He rallied some troops (the fallen angels), won them over to his cause of going against the Creator, and war became imminent in heaven.

This war was fought due to an encroachment to the throne of almighty JEHOVHA God (the forces of good). The usurper Lucifer (the forces of evil) thought he could procure the allegiance of the entire angelic hosts for the purpose of dethroning the Creator GOD. **"And there was war in heaven: Michael and his angels fought against the dragon; and the dragon fought and his angels, and prevailed not; neither was their place found any more in heaven."** Rev. 12:7 and 8

God, in His righteous might, could have destroyed the culprit, but in His infinite wisdom, He allowed sin and all that is associated with rebellion

1

to be manifested so that all creation could see the consequences of such acts along with the magnitude of His love and His grace. God had created intelligent beings, so an intellectual choice had to be made to determine which of these two entities each soul would embrace and which of the two forces would ultimately rule in their lives. Whether the forces of light over darkness, truth over lies, right over wrong, love over hate, or life over death would be determined by every intelligent being on earth. A conscientious intelligent decision must be made. The test is in place for man while the planet known as Earth became and is his 'TEST TUBE. **"But of the tree of the knowledge of good and evil, thou shalt not eat of it: for in the day that thou eatest thereof thou shalt surely die."** Gen. 2:17

The test for the first man was simply this: would he follow God at His Word, or would he, for whatever reason, disobey God and follow his own inclinations? This is the same test that is being administered today in some shape, form, or fashion by the spiritual forces that be. Will you follow God at His Word, or will you follow your own inclinations and desires instituted by Satan? This is the ultimate question and as will be examined further, these spiritual forces within this "test tube" act upon us whether we invite them to or not. They gain access into our lives in various ways from our youth up while performing daily activities, and ultimately one of them will gain the preeminence over the other (based on test results or individual choices that are made) and therefore gain the influences over the individual that is good or evil. **"To the one we are the savour of death unto death; and to the other the savour of life unto life."** 2 Cor. 2:16

At the end of a person's life, that is when death (if the life has been a child of darkness) or sleep (if it has been a child of light) comes; only one of the two forces of good and evil, whether the person was aware of it or not, would have successfully secured the worship and allegiance to the one or the other. Most will have the opportunity to make a conscientious choice. At the end of the individual's life, the total sum of choices made will have tipped the scale of God's judgment in the direction of good or evil and the question is, which one will it be? And the point to remember is, *"IT IS EITHER ONE OR THE OTHER!"* There are no in-betweens. Thus, either you will be given over to the forces of light or to the forces of darkness. At the end, your works and actions will be weighed and judged. **"For God shall bring every work [action] into judgment, with every secret thing, whether it be good, or whether it be evil."** Ecc. 12:14 **"And I heard a voice from heaven saying unto me, 'Write, Blessed are the dead which die in the Lord from henceforth:' Yea, saith the Spirit, 'that they may rest from their labours; and their works do follow them.'"** Rev. 14:13

By daily conscientious decisions made whether aware of the consequences or not, your eternal destination will be the same regardless. **"And that servant, which knew his lord's will, and prepared not himself, neither did according to his will, shall be beaten with many [stripes]. But he that knew not, and did commit things worthy of stripes, shall be beaten with few stripes."** Lk. 12:47, 48

In this Biblical scenario, both servants, he who knew and he who did not know, performed not their master's will. Therefore, both of them are punished, the former more so than the latter because he was aware of his actions. In the end, the two groups of people, those who knew to do right and those who did not know to do right, will both be judged and penalized. The one group that knew to do God's will but did it not; punishment will be a little more severe than for the group who did not know. However, both of these two groups together make up the one group that is hell bound! The other group did their Father's will and are indeed heaven bound. Amen!

Every individual is either heaven bound or hell bound based on the combined choices made over their lifetime. Heaven-bound folks are directly proportional to demonstrated practices of righteousness and inversely proportional to worldly practices. Hell-bound folks are just the opposite. They are directly proportional to worldly practices, while heavenly or Godly practices are quite small or nonexistent in their lives. In other words, seek ye first the kingdom of GOD and His righteousness. **"Ye adulterers and adulteresses, know ye not that the friendship of the world is enmity with God? Whosoever therefore will be friend of the world is the enemy of God."** Jas. 4:4

The practices that have been cherished, the secret practices that have been given exhaustive devotion and homage to, despite what has been said or done around others, it is the good or evil in the life that determines your fate. For there are many who profess to be followers of light when the actions they take appear to be more of a dark pathway rather than one of light. That is, not following the ways of the Lord. **"This people draweth nigh unto me with their mouth, and honoureth me with their lips; but their heart is far from me."** Matt. 15:8

Nevertheless again, there are conscientious choices. An intelligent decision has to be made. It would not have been something that accidentally happened. Stumbling into heaven or hell would not come by accident, not by chance nor by happenstance but a deliberate and a conscientious decision would have been made at some definitive point in each of our lives at which time spiritual probation closes. You will either be like the tree planted by the rivers of water with your roots down deep daily walking with God, or you will be like a flip-flopping fish out of water serving yourself.

Your character will either be established for good unto righteousness in CHRIST JESUS or evil unto damnation. **"He that is unjust, let him be unjust still: and he who is filthy, let him be filthy still: and he that is righteous, let him be righteous still: and he that is holy, let him be holy still."** Rev. 22:11 Your fate is sealed by which entity (Jesus or Satan) you entertain and is represented by the course of actions you take during the course of your life.

This conscientious decision-making phenomenon is primarily what separates us from the rest of the animal kingdom. Simply, the ability to make moral choices, the ability to reason, and the ability to decide right from wrong makes man of a higher order than the animals and is what basically differentiates us from them. Humans, as are all animals, are made from the lowliest and most insignificant particles on the planet—dust. **"I said in mine heart concerning the estate of the sons of men that God might manifest them, and that they might see that they themselves are beasts. For that which befalleth the sons of men befalleth beasts; even one thing befalleth them: as the one dieth, so dieth the other; yea, they have all one breath; so that man hath no preeminence above a beast: for all is vanity. All go unto one place; all are of the dust, and all turn to dust again."** Ecc. 3:18–20

Therefore, humans, along with beasts (animals), were made from particles taken from the ground and because we were born in sin and shaped in iniquity, our natural inclination is to return back to the lowliest state of being. It was only by God's plan that He gave man the ability to reason, to think, and spiritual consciousness that man was made a little lower than the angels and a little higher than the brut beasts. In other words, man could be considered the middle child, so to speak, within God's creative scheme of animated beings. 1. (Totally spiritualistic) angels, concerned mostly with things that are above; 2. (partially spiritualistic + animalistic) man, partially concerned with the things that are above and beneath; and 3. (totally animalistic) animals, concerned only with the physical that is the things that are beneath.

Considering God's creation of animated beings, angels were first, man was second, and the animals were last as far as spirituality is concerned. It is the physical side of man that God made him lower than the angels, and it is the spiritual side of man that makes him a little higher than the animals. As will be pointed out where the highest level of magnitude concerning your devotion is given to whether more to the spiritual or to the physical determines your true relationship with God or Satan.

Because of sin, it is in man's basic physical human nature to do wrong and it is this physical part of man that allows him to drag the higher order of the spiritual down to the ground. Or to put it another way, attempting to use the spiritual side to satisfy the animalistic part of man will eventually eliminate the godliness in man altogether. It was the Master's plan for man to use the spiritual to get the physical up to heaven and not the reverse of the physical, degrading the spiritual, bringing it down to hell. It is of course our sinful natural tendency to follow animalistic tendencies migrating back toward our lowest point, the dirt. **"And the LORD GOD formed man of the dust of the ground, and breathed into his nostrils the breath of life: and man became a living soul."** Gen. 2:7

In death, this physical fact is obvious. The spiritual side (breathe of life) is altogether removed, and the physical body returns to its lowest physical composition regardless if it is the desire of the body to do so or not. It does not matter whether it is buried or cremated; the human flesh will return to a handful of particles and chemicals that can be found in dirt. **"For dust thou art, and unto dust shalt thou return."** Gen. 3:19 **"All flesh shall perish together, and man shall turn again unto dust."** Job 34:15

In essence, all flesh after death, whether it is man or beast, will return to their base composition, the same elements that you would find in the earth. As will be examined further, unlike the animals, there are other attributes of man, not of the physical that God gave him that cannot be found in the soil.

In life, because man was made from dust and sin is in his nature, it is his natural humanistic tendency to use the conscientious spiritual side to think degenerate or lowly thoughts and in more cases than not, to carry out those thoughts. In other words, if a man begins to lust on women and does not attempt to control his thoughts through Christ with prayer, it is only for a short period of time that that individual will begin purchasing nudie magazines, looking at pornography on the computer, and at worst straying at night against his wife. **"And GOD saw that the wickedness of man [was]** great in the earth, and [that] every imagination of the thoughts of his heart [was] *only* evil continually. Gen. 6:5

God made man to know the good, but when he gave in to sin and became familiar with the evil, his inherited natural tendency was to do those things opposite of good, upright, and above ground because he was made from the ground, therefore his thoughts begin at once to return in that direction. Downward! With degenerate thought patterns, what else could he do but to naturally think and to do those things that point downward? Back toward the same composition of which he was made. **"Behold, I was shapened in iniquity, and in sin did my mother conceive me."** Ps. 51:5

Man has the natural tendency to pursue his vilest animalistic pleasure-loving attainments and some would do whatever to accomplish them. It is obvious that since the beginning of time, the passions of men on earth are becoming increasingly animalistic and degenerate with the increased passage of time. This degenerate behavior is becoming more tolerable and acceptable as we traverse through time because there is less sensitivity for moral right and things that are holy. It is sad to say that the human family, as time progresses, is becoming more tolerable and accepting of vice, corruption, violence, and crime; while becoming increasingly numb and desensitized to the things that are right, true, good, and wholesome. In other words, the things that are moralistically right! **"For the time will come when they <u>will not</u> endure sound doctrine; but after their own lust shall they heap to themselves teachers, having itching ears; and they shall turn away their ears from the truth, and shall be turned unto fables."** 2 Tim. 4:3 and 4 **"And God saw that the wickedness of man was great in the earth, and that <u>every imagination</u> of the thoughts of his heart was only evil <u>continually</u>."** As a matter of fact man will go far beneath the animals when it comes to moral degradation. Dogs for instance will be heterosexually attracted to other dogs regardless of class, status, or attributes of the other dog just as long as they can fulfill their sexual desires. Man on the other hand exercises the exact same principle when he hires a prostitute or goes after any woman other than his wife. But you would hardly ever see the dog having a sexual encounter with a dog of the same sexual orientation. In other words, you do not find naturally, to any measurable degree, homosexuality in the animal world. You would not see cows smooching on other cows. Many examples could be used here to show how man's thoughts and behavior actually can degrade lower than the brut beasts. Because of this and other animalistic behavior is why God said that the wickedness of man was great in the earth and that every imagination of the thoughts of his heart were only evil continually. Gen. 6:5

This is why the earth was destroyed the first time and ultimately why it will be destroyed the second time. God saw for the most part that man's thoughts were selfish, self-centered, and destructive. By the way, most sin and sinfulness falls under this general heading of selfishness. The same holds true with the statement that, **"For the love of money is the root of all evil."** 1 Tim. 6:10 Not only is the love of money the root of all evil but also all that is loved and is obtained by it. Based on the above premise, a character-defining medium had to be established; a test tube, if you will, had to be implemented to prove which of the two classes (good or evil), every one of us with moral capacity would choose and ultimately become a permanent part of.

THE TEST TUBE

In chemistry, test tubes are used to observe and test the results of a reaction between one chemical or one substance with another. In a test-tube reaction, a catalyst can be used to enhance or retard the reaction processes. The catalyst is not consumed in the reaction but after the reaction takes place, it is still in the test tube as it was before the reaction took place. A positive catalyst is used to enhance or speed up the reaction. A negative catalyst is used to hinder or slow down and possibly prevent the reaction altogether.

There are also catalysts down here in this test tube called planet Earth to interact with our reactions down here. JESUS CHRIST, the positive catalyst to retard wickedness and to enhance righteousness. **"Even the righteousness of God which is by faith of Jesus Christ unto all and upon all them that believe: for there is no difference."** Rom. 3:22

Satan, the negative catalyst, was placed here to retard righteousness and enhance wickedness. **"Therefore rejoice ye heavens, and ye that dwell in them, Woe to the inhabiters of the earth and of the sea! For the devil is come down unto you, having great wrath, because he knoweth that he hath but a short time."** Rev. 12:12

Oh, the thought of this world and how it would be if JESUS had not come! Man after sin, needed some type of constraining power or positive spiritual catalyst in his life to govern his behavior and to retard wickedness in the earth because without a positive spiritual catalyst, man would naturally sink lower and lower at a phenomenal rate! Again, because we are made from the substances of the earth without restraints, we would naturally follow the lower-negative catalyst (Satan) of selfishness, unrighteousness, and wickedness.

In this day and age, these degenerate tendencies are taking place at a very alarming rate because true or good spirituality is fading away from man and the earth. **"And the Lord said, 'My Spirit will not always strive with man, for that he also is flesh.'"** Gen. 6:3 **"But as the days of Noah were, so shall also the coming of the Son of man be."** Matt. 24:37 As God retracts His Spirit, the constraining catalyst of good, the earth grows more and more dark, man becomes more and more degenerate until the cup of God's indignation is filled to the brim. **"The same shall drink of the wine of the wrath of God, which is poured out without mixture into the cup of His indignation:"** Rev. 14:10 HE goes on to say that, **"And because iniquity shall abound, the love of many shall wax cold."** Matt. 24:12 **"For, behold, the darkness shall cover the earth, and gross darkness the people:"** Isa. 60:2

As GOD's SPIRIT is retracted from the earth, iniquity becomes more prominent, and sin like a virus begins to fill the void and attempts to take over. The human family is headed downward, and because immorality and its growth is now imperceptible, society will begin to view immoral acts as acceptable! It happens as a slow-rising flood at first unnoticeable and with acceptability becomes more apparent with time. What used to be viewed with social contempt now with the passage of time becomes the norm. This is a scary thought. Just imagine if you will, if people who have died a hundred or two hundred years ago when practiced morality was relatively high, if they could come back from the grave at this time while practicing morality is relatively low, they would probably ask to be returned to the grave. They wouldn't like it here!

There is a storehouse full of examples in nature of how things of a higher state will do their best to fall to a lower state. Let us take a look at a few of them. Waterfalls or electrical charges such as lightning are good examples of this phenomenon. In the case of naturally-flowing water, the flow will be from high pressure to low. An electrical charge will always flow from high-potential difference to a lower one, no matter how small or how great that difference is. They will always go from high to low. It does not matter whether the water is twenty thousand feet above its lowest point or two inches above; due to gravitational pull, moving water will always pursue the lower point. The same is true with electricity. Whether the differences of the potential are twenty thousand volts or two mV (two millivolts), the charge will always follow the path from high- to low-potential difference. Never under natural circumstances will you see the reverse being true. A rock pushed off of a high cliff or a low hill will always go from high ground to low. You would never observe water, electricity, or a rock going from a low to high pressure or potential difference unless there is some other external force causing them to do so. Another example of this is, if an opened bottle of perfume is placed on a table in the middle of a room, it is only a matter of time before the smell of it reaches the four corners of the room because the aromatic molecules of the perfume will attempt to fill the entire room. The aroma will attempt to go from an area of high concentration, where the opened bottle was placed, to an area of low concentration that is over a wider area in the room.

Again, in a chemical reaction, the reactants will almost always go to a less volatile position from a high- to a low-energy state or to its most stable position. So man also, if not controlled by some higher law or principle, would have a tendency to gravitate toward a lower point that is our vilest or most basic animalistic state.

Could you imagine what this planet would be like if man did not have certain moral, constitutional, and civil laws to govern him? Go ahead, take a moment and try to imagine it. It's kind of scary, isn't it? There would unquestionably be anarchy. That is law unto self—every man doing what seems right in his own eyes. Most would agree that because of sin, we as a sinful human family would be pretty bad off. Just think of the crimes; murders, rapes, robberies, thefts, lying, and cheating! In some cities of the earth, the numbers are pretty high today even with laws in place, but think how it would be if there were none! And just like mathematical, chemical, and physical laws are in place to govern nature, we too need laws to govern us!

The great God of heaven saw through His infinite wisdom the need for moral laws to govern His universe by way of the Ten Commandments. He would not have been a good God if He left it to man to come up with and establish the only laws that exist. It would have been a perfect mess! But if there were no laws initially given by God, things would truly be a perfect mess! Nevertheless, even with these laws in place, over time it is still man's natural tendency to slide on a downward path to moral and civil degradation and degeneracy. **"Because sentence against an evil work is not executed speedily, therefore the heart of the sons of men is fully set in them to do evil."** Ecc. 8:11

THE LAW OF LOVE
(THE TEN COMMANDMENTS)

L et us consider the moral laws of God (the Ten Commandments). Notice the first four are attributed to God Himself. This is reasonable so that there would not be any doubt as to who God is and how He wishes us (His created beings) to respect, honor, and worship Him. The last six are for man's benefit. This too is reasonable because God shows man how to live together with respect for each other and their property. God could have taken 100 percent of all the commandments and made them only for Himself. He did not have to give man anything. Instead, He being the unselfish God that He is took only 40 percent and left 60 percent of them for our personal welfare with peace on earth and goodwill toward men. Amen.

Unlike the Dark Ages when governments attempted to dictate religious conscience within today's society in this country, there are no civil laws being enforced to govern the first four of the Ten Commandments pertaining to God. This is justifiably so because God never forces His will and worship upon anyone, and therefore religion or worship within governments should not be forced by governments. However, God would love to see a government and entire nation follow Him completely at His will. Nevertheless, this is not the case, not on this planet.

The only society where it may be said that God's true way and the entire Ten Commandment Law including the first four pertaining to God and the last six pertaining to your neighbor was ever attempted to be enforced was within the Jewish law or society. It needs to be made clear that the enforcement and the penalties established with breaking these laws were given by Moses and thus termed Moses's law and not to be confused with the Law of the Covenant or the Ten Commandment Law. The Law of the Covenant (the Ten Commandment Law) was given by God and written with His finger. The law of Moses or Moses's law was conceptually idealized and formulated around the Law of the Covenant. It was set up by him as a civil law to attempt to keep the Jewish people on track with the Law of the Covenant, the Ten Commandments; God's Universal Law that is immutable. In other words, for the purposes of enforcing God's law, Moses gave his people some parameters for keeping this law. And as widely known from the scriptures, time after time even from the onset, the children did not very well keep any of the laws pertaining to neither God nor their fellow man the way they should have kept them. They did not keep GOD's Ten Commandment Law nor did they keep Moses's law the way God or Moses had intended. **"Do not think that I will accuse you to the Father: there is one that accuses you, even Moses, in whom you trust. For had you believed Moses, you would have believed Me; for he wrote of Me. But if you believe not his writings, how should you believe My words?"** Jn. 5:45–47

However, in almost every society on this planet, even in remote jungles, there are laws or norms in place to enforce almost all the six moral laws God gave us that pertain to fellow man. There are civil laws pertaining to murder or killing, stealing, perjury or lying, cheating on one's spouse, etc. If you were to check out some states' law archives, you would find that most of them have some outdated laws on their law books concerning the act of committing adultery because in times past, the morality of this society was at a higher level than it is today. However, this law of committing adultery today is hardly being enforced or not being enforced at all because a higher percentage of people are committing it, even those who are commissioned

14

to uphold the law. Our society has degraded so far that actually violating this particular law is almost viewed as today's societal norm. You are almost viewed as strange if you do not behave in this manner. Have you ever noticed also within our society that a high-ranking official can get caught cheating on his/her spouse and may only get a slight reprimand for it? A smack on the wrist if that! Most times than not, they get to continue in their office. But let them get caught killing someone or stealing money from the office. They would most certainly lose their position and possibly get prison time. In other words, where are our values really being placed today? Is it mostly on material goods and only very violent crimes?

God's moral laws that are not enforced by civil laws will always be the first to go. In most societies, no one is paying much attention to them. The person who is messing around sexually behind their spouse's back. Or the people who are messing around sexually and are not even married! Except for some entertaining gossip, judges, governments, and societies as a whole could care less! Some might even relish in the thought of doing it themselves!

Let's consider as mentioned above a state law concerning the seventh commandment of GOD's moral law (Ten Commandments) which deals with committing adultery. If properly researched, you'd find that most states do not enforce it. Thus, more often than what you could ever suppose, people are breaking this law at an alarming rate, not to mention fornication (the act of having sex between two unmarried people). Again, even by people who are in positions to uphold the law of the land, this particular moral law is being severely abused. Not to even mention those who should be upholding a straight testimony and the word of God (pastors, priests, and other clergy)!

Even though committing adultery is an offense both to God and one's fellow man, this law deals with lustful pleasure-seeking corruption, and many are willfully breaking this law with little being done to curb it. Therefore, this particular moral law is broken time and time again because there appears to be no immediate penalty for the offense. It satisfies the lusts and most times than not, lies, deception, and even assault are associated with it. It is also one of the first moral laws of the six dealing with our fellow man, broken or not kept. Although there may not be a record of this act or an immediate price to pay here on earth, there is, however, an accurate record kept on high and a definite price to pay at the end of time. **"Blessed are they that do His Commandments that they may have right to the tree of life, and may enter in through the gates into the city. For without are dogs, and sorcerers, and whoremongers, and murderers, and idolaters, and whomsoever loveth and maketh a lie."** Rev.22:14 and 15

This heavenly record keeping is by far better than the best computers we have down here. There are no mistakes in this bookkeeping journal. No earthly mortal falsely accused and penalized for something they did not do. You may be able to fool some people and may even fool yourself by thinking you have gotten away with something, but nothing is obscure from the all-seeing eye of Almighty God. **"And I beheld, and, lo, in the midst of the throne and of the four beasts, and in the midst of the elders, stood a Lamb as it had been slain, having seven horns and seven eyes, which are the seven Spirits of God sent forth into all the earth."** Rev. 5:6

Now on the other hand, the sixth law of the moral law of God *is* included and enforced by the civil laws of man. The moral law commandment "Thou shalt not kill" is not only on the books of states' laws but is judiciously enforced by the state. Let us be clear though; with all the murders and killings that take place in our land, the breaking of this sixth law is minuscule compared to the breaking of the seventh (that is the committing of adultery/fornication). Why? Because of moral degradation, it is more tolerated and accepted. Moral laws that are not civilly enforced by man will be committed more frequently with moral degradation expanding at an exponential rate until the end of time. This is the very reason why atheism/disbelief in God (Thou shalt have no other gods before Me.), idol worship (Thou shalt not make unto thee any graven image), degrading the name of God (Thou shalt not take the name of the Lord thy God in vain), not keeping the Sabbath day holy (Remember the Sabbath day to keep it Holy), dishonoring parents (Honor thy father and thy mother), committing adultery/fornication (Thou shalt not commit adultery), lying and cheating (Thou shalt not bear false witness against thy neighbor), and lusting/coveting (Thou shalt not covet). In other words, the moral laws least enforced or not enforced by the civil laws of man are quickly and frequently infringed upon by the human race, and most times the temptation is given into when the sin avails itself. Trespassing against these moral laws will continue to increase and thus cause moral degradation within our society to expand at a greater rate as time passes. As can be seen by today's violence (murders, rape, robberies, etc.), the ones that are enforced will also increase but not as rapidly as the ones that are not.

With increased law enforcement, prisons, and technology, you would think that crime at some point would decline and altogether disappear. However, this is not the case. This philosophy and practice simply has not holistically deterred crime. Since the beginning of time, crime rates continue to increase from age to age and seem to become more violent. As God and His standards are removed from the scene, more and more darkness seeps in until love, mercy, and true justice all but seem to vanish. **"And because iniquity shall abound the love of many shall wax cold."** Matt. 24:12

An atheist is a person who does not believe in God. There are more atheists today than at any other time in this Earth's history. Back in ancient times [Some people say back in Bible times as opposed to ancient times, as if we have already entered into the new Earth. However, we are still living in Bible times until the end of time.], most people in ancient cultures believed in some form of god even if it was the wrong one. Though many of them were graven images made by the hands of man, they had some false god to worship. Check out how the word of God pokes a little pun at them, **"Then the wood-carver measures a block of wood and draws a pattern on it. He works with chisel and plane and carves it into a human figure. He** gives it human beauty and puts it in a little shrine. He cuts down cedars; he selects the cypress and the oak; he plants the pine in the forest to be nourished by the rain. Then he uses part of the wood to make a fire. With it he warms himself and bakes his bread. Then-yes, it's true-he takes the rest of it and makes himself a god to worship! He makes an idol and bows down in front of it! He burns part of the tree to roast his meat and to keep himself warm. He says, 'Ah, that fire feels good.' Then he takes what's left and makes his god: a carved idol! He falls down in front of it, worshiping and praying to it. 'Rescue me!' he says. 'You are my god!' Such stupidity and ignorance! Their eyes are closed, and they cannot see. Their minds are shut, and cannot think. The person who made the idol never stops to reflect, 'Why, it's just a block of wood! I burned half of it for heat and used it to bake my bread and roast my meat. How can the rest of it be a god? Should I bow down to worship a piece of wood?'" Isa. 44:13–19 (NLT) There is however, one true God, and HE is the supplier of the moral laws. The very first commandment of GOD's moral laws is, **"I am the LORD; Thou shalt have no other gods before ME."** EX 20:3 and 4

As mentioned before, in ancient times, most cultures and the peoples of those cultures had some form of theological worship. That is that their societies were centered on the belief and worship of some type of deistic form. Again, even if it was the wrong one, they had a god or gods in their social structure. Not so today! Due to a lack of faith, more and more people are saying that there is no God and that they are going to trust in intellectual knowledge, academia, man's capabilities, science, and reason. No matter how much wealth, education, or worldly status a person may have, the sacred scriptures declare, **"The fool hath said in his heart, 'There is no God.'"** Ps. 14:1

An even worse scenario is in the case of nominal Christians who claim to believe in God do so only with their mouths and do not with their hearts. This is dangerous because claims are made with their mouths that they are saved Christians but actually their feelings, thoughts, and behaviors are much similar to the atheist and agnostics placing their trust in man more so than in God. Little time is spent in devotion to God, and they make pretense to call on God when it is convenient, as in a social gathering (church) or when in trouble. This only makes them more hypocritical than the atheist or unbeliever. The atheists and unbelievers are holistically disassociated with God not professing Him while living a life indicative of such; while the unsanctified believer hypocritically proclaims God with their mouth only, but their deportments and actions point more in the worldly or unbeliever's direction. **"This people draweth nigh unto me with their mouths, and do honoureth me with their lips; but their heart is far from me."** Matt. 15:8 Therefore it is definitely not nearly enough to profess GOD with the lips while the heart is not right with HIM.

We now live in a society that has extracted the Ten Commandments, prayer, and any form of holiness out of the classrooms of public schools for our children. But in this same society, you can find adult bookstores and entertainment, topless and bottomless nudie bars, liquor stores and nightclubs on almost every other corner. You can find stories of wizardry, witchcraft, homosexuality, all types of gangster rap, violent computer games, and any other mess you can think of in our public and in some private schools.

Innocent children are placed in the care of perverts, homosexuals, atheists, and immoral nitwits every time they are sent off to these schools. Parents and care providers don't have a clue who these administrators, educators, or support staffs of these schools are, nor what or who they represent that are teaching these children and it is the parents or guardians, the very ones who should be protecting them, that sends them there! It is almost like trusting them to perfect strangers. Of course, not all of our educators are this way, but who is to say who is and who is not. But know this, that Satan is the arch-deceiver, the master of deception and will not leave any institution especially one that deals with young minds to pure and holy teachings and the right way for them without making a serious effort to dislodge and ultimately destroy them spiritually. This is the very reason why prayer, the Ten Commandments, and holiness in general are not in the classroom. It is basically of Satan's design for it to be this way. This is a major concept of Satan used in part to prevent the young mind from seeing Jesus but adhering to the things and cares of the world at an early age, and he has been working on this for thousands of years. **"Be sober, be vigilant; because your adversary the devil, as a roaring lion walketh about, seeking whom he may devour."** 1 Pet. 5:8 **"And his tail drew the third part of the stars of heaven, and did cast them to the earth: and the dragon stood before the woman which was ready to be delivered, for to devour her child as soon as it was born."** Rev. 12:4 If the enemy was there to devour the Messiah as soon as He was born, what do you think he has instituted and set up to devour your child as soon as they are born? Not so much as to kill them physically, though some times that is the case, but to bring them down spiritually from birth to adulthood.

Do not believe for one moment the archenemy will leave innocent children alone! He is after them with full demonic spiritual force! And most of the time it begins within the public school system, if not at home. If he has crept into the church (which he has), it is also necessary to believe that he has not only crept into but has a high stake in the public school system or any school system for that matter. **"And the great dragon was cast out, that old serpent, called the Devil, and Satan, *which deceiveth the whole world*: he was cast out into the earth, and his angels were cast out with him."** Rev. 12:9 **"Therefore rejoice ye heavens, and ye that dwell in them. Woe to the inhabiters of the earth and of the sea! For the devil is come down unto you, having great wrath, because he knoweth that he hath but a short time."** Rev. 12:12

For the most part, it is allowable for ungodly people to teach children, but the children are not allowed to pray in the classroom! They can, however, read books like Harry Potter and other articles on wizardry, astrology, witchcraft, black magic, and sorcery. They are encouraged to look at, read, and listen to things that are related to and consisting of spiritualism and mysticism. Not to mention books on sex, drugs, crimes, and other demoralizing garbage, but they cannot read the *BIBLE in class*! Something is gravely wrong with this picture!

Most people consider themselves to be intelligent mature adults and trust their children to the care of these closet characters and perverts that may be within the school systems. They do not consider that the Bible is the best book to teach not only our children but demoralized adults as well. It is an outstanding source to teach and reteach them moral ethics and high standards of living in righteousness toward a living GOD and toward our fellow man. **"And thou shalt love the Lord thy God with all thine heart, and with all thy soul, and with all thy might. And these words, which I command thee this day, shall be in thine heart: And thou shalt teach them diligently unto thy children, and shalt talk of them when thou sittest in thine house, and when thou walkest by the way, and when thou liest down, and when thou riseth up."** Deut. 6:5–7

There is absolutely nothing in the Bible instructing anyone to do any negativism, wrongs, or harm to anyone else. As a matter of fact, it is quite the contrary. The word of God instructs to love at all costs, to be unselfish, and to not get tired of well doing. These are simple and wholesome concepts that it would be well to teach not children only but all humanity as well. **"But I say unto you, Love your enemies, bless them that curse you, do good to them that hate you, and pray for them which despitefully use you, and persecute you."** Matt. 5:44 For example, this and other similar texts could be used at school to instruct the schoolhouse bully and those kids who enjoy picking on other students.

Children are gladly sent off by parents to these synagogues of Satan called public schools and state-run universities! This planet is in trouble! Note also that institutions of higher learning such as a university are segmented into integral parts that make up the complex whole. Each department feverishly seeks to obtain the highest level of knowledge possible. They are funded by governments for research and development. With each integral part (departments) feverishly attempting to attain the highest level of knowledge that can be reached and that my friend pertains to God alone. If each department of the institution could attain to the highest level of knowledge and come together as a universal whole they would attempt to sit on earth as all-knowing God. This is ultimately what they seek but will never attain. It is impossible for man to do.

Nevertheless, moral degradation continues to take a severe plunge even with increased knowledge all while God has attempted to reconcile man back to Himself at the cross. This degradation took place imperceptibly slow at first. Remember, the devil is very deceptive. He will steal your soul if you let him.

Some of us not of the younger generation can remember growing up watching prime-time television programs of days gone by. (Younger people would not have a clue.) The married couples were shown sleeping in separate twin beds and fully clothed in pajamas. Shows like *The Dick Van Dyke Show,* and *My Three Sons,* and *Leave it to Beaver,* and *I Love Lucy.* Do you remember? The parents always slept in separate twin beds fully clothed. Also, any foul language or curse words that may have been mentioned on night or comedy shows, no matter how small or insignificant, were censored, bleeped out, or omitted altogether. Most times, they were omitted. Again, not so today! Today, a child can come home from school, turn on the TV, and see unmarried and/or married men and women, men and men, and/or women and women climbing in and out of the same bed naked. No clothes on at all, with hardly anything uncensored! Children can hear four-letter words right on regular broadcasting, not to mention cable TV and the falsehoods of so-called cartoons. Some parents let this mess on TV babysit their children while they are taking care of other business. It is an eternal mistake to let your children watch those so-called cartoons also. With the violence and suggestive materials in some of them they become worse than some adult programs and should be rated X or XX. Most of them today have other underlying messages in them, even if suggestive material is not readily seen. If there is not spiritualism or violence, there is something else that is not good for young minds hidden in the script. We are in trouble on every side, and every individual who is seeking peace need to turn around and react with the truth and follow righteousness. Amen. Turn neither to the right nor to the left but straight into the Kingdom of GOD!

One reason for this downward spiral is because man almost always looks at the laws in place to see where he can get around a particular law in question or to see if he can find a loophole to not confer holistically with that law. Most of us conscientiously try to look for the best way to benefit ourselves during business dealings or such as when we file our taxes. Most people will try to find loopholes whenever they will best benefit their situation. Some will even at times lie when it is convenient or monetarily gainful.

Civil laws of a society usually deal with the last part of God's entire moral laws (the Ten Commandments) which basically focuses on sins or crimes against our fellow man in society, and penalties have been established to deter violation of these laws. However, concerning civil laws as noted above places more focus on only two of the moral laws of God. They are the ones dealing with the laws of our fellow man and that of killing/murders (Thou shalt not kill) and stealing, taking something from someone that does not belong to you (Thou shalt not steal). But for the most part, people often go against the first part of the Ten Commandments and when they can get away with it, will break the last part of God's moral law as well. Except for the two laws mentioned (killing and stealing), people lie, cheat, commit adultery, covet, and do not honor their parents at will.

Let us consider breaking the speed limit for instance. This is a civil law not of God's Ten Commandment Law, established by man to protect one's self and others. Most people have intentionally gone over the speed limit when they were somewhat in a hurry. They were conscientiously aware of the fact when they did it. It was done on purpose. Some people also have broken this law unintentionally. Whether aware of it or not, the law was still broken, and consequentially one should be penalized for the offense whether they got away with it or not. They should go down to the courthouse and pay the fine (especially if they are Christian). I ask you, how many of us will voluntarily do that? When realization occurs and you know you are over the speed limit, the right thing to do is not wait until a ticket is received but to go down and voluntarily pay the fine for the penalty of the committed crime. That is paying the price for speeding over the limit. Getting caught by the highway trooper brings you into a realistic awareness that you have broken the law. You broke the law got caught and now are sorrowful or angry that you got caught! But if the trooper does not stop you, there is a feeling of getting away with something. It will be soon forgotten that you have committed an unlawful act against society and your fellow man. Also, it needs to be pointed out that if you get away with something the first time, there is a high probability that at some point, you will try it again a second time. While driving down the highway notice how many people are driving over the limit and some of them accept their higher speed as the norm and feel as if they are doing nothing against the law.

We inherently cannot help ourselves against sin for even at a very early age, it comes to all naturally. A child, for instance, takes a cookie from the proverbial cookie jar, with the telltale markings of the chocolate crumbs all around his mouth and possibly a cookie or two still in each hand, with the cookie jar lying on the floor. "Johnny, did you go into the cookie jar?" his mother asks from the next room. "No, not me!" little Johnny replies. First, he stole the cookies or took them without permission, then he had the ability to lie about his actions and have not had a single lesson in stealing nor lying 101, but he was able to carry out both parts of the sin with accuracy, precision, and at a very early age without being taught. Why? Because of natural tendency—the innate ability to follow the moralistically downward path. **"Behold, I was shapen in iniquity; and in sin did my mother conceive me."** Ps. 51:5

As you continue onward down the pathway of life, you will find everything that you say and/or do is either directly or indirectly supportive of one of these two entities: good or evil, right or wrong, just or unjust, holy or unholy, Christ or Satan. So to put it simply, this phenomenon known as life can be viewed as the test while planet Earth is the test tube. Our lifelong experiences, every act, every deed, and every word are being observed and recorded by higher powers, and our earthly existence is our reaction medium. **"For God shall bring every work into judgment, with every secret thing, whether it be good, or whether it be evil."** Ecc. 12:14 **"For by thy words thou shalt be justified, and by thy words thou shalt be condemned."** Matt. 12:37

Ultimately, how a person plays or act out their test-tube experience will permanently decide what base material they are made of, or to phrase it another way, in the end, it will tell whose servant you truly are. In the end, will it be that you are found to be a degenerate sludgy metal or as gold tried in the fire.

On the surface, you can say and do almost anything you want and have a squeaky-clean appearance, but what you say and do when you feel no one is watching is where the true heart lies. **"For the Lord seeth not as man seeth; for man looketh on the outward appearance, but the Lord looketh on the heart."** 1 Sam. 16:7

It is not enough to go to church in pious-looking attire and through the rest of the week doing everything that a true Christian should not do. Remember that sin is the reason for this test-tube experience. If Adam and Eve had passed the first test, there would have never been a need for another test. But because of sin, everyone has to go through the fiery trials of temptation and testing to see what they are really made of. And since we are being tested here on this planet, it is therefore reasonable to claim this world as a test tube or testing center where the rest of the universe is intently watching to see how this reaction will play out and who will come forth, as gold tried in the fire.

God forever wants us to be on His side, but He allows Satan to try or to test us to see if we really belong there. And, my friend, where your eternal destination will be is determined by what base material you are. Either a child of God in Christ Jesus or of Satan, life or death, heaven or hell, *there are no* other choices. There is no straddling the fence or walking the middle line. You will be, and even now is, on one side or the other. However, it is my sincere desire that every sincere reader of this book will consider their place and choose good over evil, life over death, and subsequently Christ over the cares of this world and Satan.

As you prayerfully read this book, please take careful consideration of where you stand at this point in time as this earth's history rapidly comes to its conclusion. The eternal hope is that you will end on the spiritual side of right. **"And be not conformed to this world: but be ye transformed by the renewing of your mind to do what is that good and acceptable, and perfect will of God."** Rom. 12:2 "This is your reasonable service!"

Sin

Since sin originated in the early recesses of the beginning of time and is the primary reason why our environmental test tube exists as it does today, it would be appropriate to expound on this mysterious and destructive phenomenon. Let us begin by defining sin. Where did it come from and why? The biblical definition of sin is, **"Whosoever committeth sin transgresseth also the law:** _for sin is the transgression of the law._**"** ☒1 Jn. 3:4

This is the biblical definition of sin: Sin is the transgression of the law. Sin is any and every thing that is either directly or indirectly opposing the will of God. Not following God's WORD is sin. To put it simply, the Ten Commandments, (God's moral law) expresses God's character and His divine will for His created beings with moral capabilities. All created beings known to man, other than angels and man himself, does not have the ability of moral choice. Therefore, their will was imposed upon them in this world but not moral beings such as man and angels as a preprogrammed animated species. In other words, a cat cannot sin. A horse cannot sin. A lion cannot sin. Animals cannot intentionally transgress God's law and therefore commit sin.

Let us examine to a small degree which law we are referring to that causes a created moral agent to sin. There are mainly two laws that come into question when we refer to the laws concerning the scriptures and subsequently the main two that most people are confused about when the Bible talks about such things as the law being nailed to the cross. First and foremost, all references referring to God's law or the law of God are pointing toward His UNIVERSAL LAW, THE TEN COMMANDMENTS, His moral law for created moral agents (God's law). This law was established not at Mount Sinai and given to the Jews for only their benefit as many people believe or express. Quite the contrary, the Ten Commandment Laws were in effect since the beginning of time and will be throughout eternity. Before there was ever a Jew, the law of God existed. **"Jesus said unto them, 'Verily, verily, I say unto you, Before Abraham was, I Am.'"** John 8:58

Again, the Ten Commandment Law is a transcript of God's unchanging character. This law governs the entire universe and is therefore often referred to as God's UNIVERSAL LAW. That is, the entire universe is governed by this Law of the Creator God.

Now the second law in question would be the Law of Moses or Moses's law. These primarily consisted of the instructions Moses gave the children of Israel to assist them in living right and to help them not to infringe upon God's moral laws, how to function within their economy, how to treat one another; how to worship God, etc. For example, if a woman was caught in the act of adultery, Moses's Law explicitly states she should be stoned to death. The law of the adulterous act is still very much in effect today as it was in Moses's day because it is part of God's Universal Law. "Thou shalt not commit adultery." This law was not nailed to the cross as many believe or would like for it to be. However, the penalty for committing the act, the law of stoning to death (Moses's law) is of none effect today. Moses's law for the penalty of committing adultery was the stoning to death of the one committing the act. This, however, was nailed to the cross. Is that clear? Also, as we all know, the sacrificial laws concerning the slaying of animals for the atonement of sin were also nailed to the cross. The blood of animals cannot and never could atone for the sins of man. But the wages of sin is and always has been death. **"For the wages of sin is death."** Rom. 6:23

Christ the Messiah had not come in Ancient Israel's or Moses's day, but the wages of sin was still death. The sacrifice of the animals, as we will discuss later, pointed toward the true sacrifice of Jesus Christ. We no longer have to fulfill these rituals because Christ has paid it all for us. **"And all that dwell upon the earth shall worship Him, whose names are not written in the book of life of the Lamb slain from the foundation of the world."** Rev. 13:8

These were the laws Moses instructed them to live by and to place on the side of the Ark of the Covenant. **"Take this book of the law, and put it in the side of the ark of the covenant of the LORD your God, that it may be there for a witness against you."** Deut. 31:26

Please note that this law was not placed inside the ark as was God's Ten Commandment Law. They were two distinguishable and separate sets of laws. (1) the law inside the Ark of the Covenant—God's Universal Ten Commandment Law written with the finger of God, and (2) the law on the side of the Ark of the Covenant—Moses's law, a law for instruction.

Another thing about Moses's Law to note is that this law could be modified by misinterpretation either by the high priests, rabbi, kings, and others who may be in authority. Often, this was the case by Pharisees and Sadducees, supposedly keepers of the law. In one instance, Jesus was healing a man on the seventh-day Sabbath; some of the leaders of the day accused Him of breaking it. Jesus handled the situation by saying, **"And answered them saying, 'Which of you shall have an ass or an ox fallen into a pit, and will not straightway pull him out on the Sabbath day?'"** Lk 14:5

Jesus went on to say that it was okay to do well on the Sabbath Day. The Pharisees had altered the law so badly as to say that if a bucket of water was carried or travelling beyond a certain distance by foot was considered work. In other words if your mother was sick out in the country and you had to carry a bucket of water from the spring some distance beyond the allowable distance to minister to your mother or a friend for that matter, you would have been considered working and you need not do it or be stoned!

According to the law as they had made it to say, "Just leave her sick and possibly die until the Sabbath is past." This is not what Jesus or Moses for that matter were teaching nor intended. Is it important to keep the Sabbath Holy as God instructed in His Universal Law? Sure it is. Is God's law done away with? Certainly it is not. Is it okay to do well on the Sabbath Day? Sure it is. Not to deliberately break the Sabbath doing anything for personal gain but to do well in it. If any activity is being done on the Sabbath day for self-gratification or self-gain then it is not being kept holy as the Lord Himself commanded. "Remember the Sabbath Day, to keep it Holy." Exo.20:8 To make it clearer, if you vainly go shopping on the Sabbath to satisfy your lust for worldly fashions then you are not keeping the Sabbath holy. You are satisfying self. However, if you go shopping on the Sabbath to clothe a homeless person or for some other act reflecting Jesus, then it is impossible for you to be breaking the Sabbath. You are in very deed keeping it holy.

Evidence shows that things became cloudy and confused when men began to put his two cents into something. The very ones who should have been upholding the law were interpreting it falsely to make themselves appear pious and holy. When in all actuality, they were not keeping the law the way Moses intended them to and they were corrupting it. **"For had you believed Moses, you would have believed Me; for he wrote of Me. But if you believe not his writings, how shall you believe My words?"** Jn. 5:46 and 47

The distinction of the two laws should now be clearer. There should not now be any confusion as to which law we are referring to when we discuss the Law of the Covenant (Ten Commandments) and the Law of Moses. It was the Law of Moses that pointed toward the coming Messiah. It was *this* law that is fulfilled in Christ and was ultimately nailed to the cross. **"Blotting out the handwriting of ordinances that was against us, which was contrary to us, and took it out of the way, nailing it to His cross."** Col. 2:14

The Law of the Covenant, God's law consisting of the Ten Commandments can never be done away with. For this is the Law of the Covenant that God

Himself established between Him and man, therefore, it continues on until the great trumpet sounds and time ceases to exist. Christ Himself felt the need to make this point clear when He said, **"Think not that I am come to destroy the law, or the prophets: I am not come to destroy, but to fulfill; For verily I say unto you, Till heaven and earth pass, one jot or one tittle shall in no wise pass from the law, till all be fulfilled."** Matt. 5:17 and 18 This is in reference to the Ten Commandment Law, not the law of ordinances that were later nailed to the cross at Jesus's crucifixion.

Also, let us be clear of the fact that the Ten Commandment moral law is in effect whether you are on Earth, on the moon, on Jupiter, in another galaxy, or wherever you are in the entire universe. It does not matter where you are in God's vast universe. The plan of redemption that is the implemented plan that required a cross only pertained to planet Earth. There are other unfallen worlds where God's Universal Law simply could not have been nailed to the cross. **"And it shall come to pass, that from one new moon to another, and from one Sabbath to another, shall all flesh come to worship before Me, saith the LORD."** Isa. 66:23 Even under the sea, His law is in effect. **"Whither shall I go from thy Spirit? Or whither shall I flee from thy presence? If I ascend up into heaven, thou art there: if I make my bed in hell, behold, thou art there. If I take the wings of the morning, and dwell in the uttermost parts of the sea; Even there shall thy hand lead me, and thy right hand shall hold me."** Ps.139 7-10 **"Canst thou by searching find out God? Canst thou find out the Almighty unto perfection? It is as high as heaven; what canst thou do? Deeper than hell; what canst thou know?"** Job 11:7 and 8

It is this unchanging law that was written and given to Moses by God Himself placing it *inside* the Ark of the Covenant. There it abode beneath the mercy seat of God with the cherubs reverently looking downward toward it while their wings were outstretched on high. This is the Law of the Covenant and the breaking or transgressing of it, as was shown earlier, is what defines sin.

Again, to break any *one* of the Ten Commandments is a direct inducement of sin or opposition to the will of God. **"For whosoever shall keep the whole law, and yet offend in one point, he is guilty of all."** Jam. 2:10

It is a package deal. The ten exists as if they were one! Violation of any one of the Ten Commandment Law is not the same as the breaking of one of our civil laws. The penalties for violating one of our civil laws vary according to the magnitude of the crime and what the earthly judge wishes to impose. On the other hand, there is only one penalty with the breaking of any part of the unified Law of the Covenant—death! **"For the wages of sin is death."** Rom. 6:23 **and sin is the transgression of the Law!**

However, unlike the earthly judges, the Heavenly Judge has a way of pardoning all who accepts and follows Him at His word. **"But the gift of God is eternal life through Jesus Christ our Lord."** Rom. 6:23 The judges here on earth hardly ever pardons anyone, much less a hardened criminal, but praise be to God; we can all be forgiven, even the harden criminal, because the price has been paid for all who will come to Him by our Lord Jesus Christ. Amen. Jesus paid the price that we just simply could not have paid! Remember, *"There is a fountain filled with blood drawn from Emmanuel's veins and sinners plunge beneath that flood lose all their guilty stains. The dying thief rejoiced to see that fountain in his day; and there may I though vile as he wash all my sins away."* hymnal If Christ could save that guilty thief, then surely He can save any other guilty sinner. **"For all have sinned and fall short of the glory of God."** Rom. 3:23

One other important aspect concerning the law that needs to be pointed out is this: to place a stumbling block before your brother, causing him to fail or to go against the express will of God, is an indirect fulfillment of sin. In other words, the one causing the sin as well as the one who commits the sin both are guilty. **"Whosoever therefore shall break one of these least** commandments, <u>and</u> shall teach men so, shall be called the least in the Kingdom of Heaven: but whosoever shall do <u>and</u> teach them shall be called great in the Kingdom of Heaven." Matt. 5:19

Whether you are actually committing the sinful act intentionally or unintentionally, directly or indirectly, teaching others to go against God to break His Ten Commandment Law either way, it is sin. It is in opposition to the coherent will of the highest power (God). When sin is committed, it is subjected to the consequences of that opposition which will ultimately be reviewed and dealt with at the end of time. The one who opposed God by transgressing His law is the one by default who should pay for the offense. However, praise be to God, if the one who is truly guilty turns with true repentance to the true Lamb of God, then the one who should have truly died will be truly forgiven and truly saved by the blood of Jesus Christ. Amen!

Those who are in pulpits across the country and around the world teaching error with zeal or otherwise are in violation of God's law according to Matthew 5:19. It must be recognized by all that God is a pure and holy form. He has a *zero* tolerance for sin. **"For whosoever shall keep the whole law, and yet offend in one point, he is guilty of all."** James 2:10

Illustrating this point another way is if a person does not commit adultery but is rooted in lies or covetousness (sins that are not readily noticeable), that person might as well commit them all because according to the Word of God, if one point is offended, you have offended them all. This is why it is important to walk in the perfectiveness and the newness of life in Christ Jesus. **"Therefore we are buried with Him by baptism into death: that like as Christ was raised up from the dead by the glory of the Father, even so we also should walk in newness of life."** Rom. 6:4 **"Be ye therefore perfect, even as your Father which is in heaven is perfect."** Matt. 5:48

Recognition at the exact moment when the temptation to commit sin arises is essential for the tempted one to have a good chance to resist. **"Submit yourselves therefore unto God, resist the devil and he will flee**

from you." James 4:7 If the sin is committed, it will bring forth death. **"Then when lust hath conceived, it bringeth forth sin: and sin, when finished, bringeth forth death."** James 1:15

Though the penalty for sin is often not administered right away, sin after committing it does not simply evaporate into thin air as most believe after committing them. Often people forget the sinful act almost as soon as it is completed. Kind of like a person beholding their face in a mirror. Not much longer after looking into the mirror they walk away from it they forget what they look like. That is the very reason why five minutes later they are back in the mirror taking another look as if something has changed. **"For if any be a hearer of the word, and not a doer, he is like unto a man beholding his natural face in a glass: For he beholdeth himself, and goeth his way, and straightway forgetteth what manner of man he was."** James 1:23 and 24

Certainly, the penalty of the sinful act, whether it is a little lie or a big idolatry, is not necessarily administered right there on the spot. In most cases, a person that goes against the will of God does not fall down and die right there on the spot as seen happening in some cases in the Old Testament. This is simply because God is long-suffering. Therefore, the offender often feels as if they have gotten away with the sinful deed even though they have the knowledge of doing wrong. That is because the penalty of the sinful act is hardly ever administered right there on the spot. The transgressor of GOD's law (the sinner) deserves to die or pay for his/her sin or sins right there on the spot but because of the grace, mercy, and long-suffering of God, the sinner is often given chance after chance after chance to come back to God and to get it right with Him. **"And the LORD passed by before him, and proclaimed, 'The LORD, The LORD God, merciful and gracious, longsuffering, and abundant in goodness and truth. Keeping mercy for thousands, forgiving iniquity and transgression and sin, and that will by no means clear the guilty; visiting the iniquity of the fathers upon the children, and upon the children's children, unto the third and to the fourth generation.'"** Ex. 34:6

and 7 (We need to remember tough that He shows mercy unto thousands of them who love Him and keep His commandments [Ex. 20:6.])

Because God has a zero tolerance for sin, blood atonement must be made for the sinful deed no matter how small, and by rights the sinner should pay with his own blood. But again, because the penalty for sin is not exacted right there on the spot, most sinners have a sense of committing a wrong to their self-gratifying pleasure and getting away with it. However, we all well know that every sinful act committed will be dealt with at the last day in judgment. **"He that rejecteth Me, and receiveth not My words, hath one that judgeth him: the word that I have spoken, the same shall judge him in the last day."** Jn. 12:48

Let us view an analogy of disappearing sin compared to the evaporation of water. Like the evaporation of water, committed sin appears to disappear. However, this is not the case. On a hot sunny summer's day, you can pour a glass of water on your front porch or sidewalk as you go to work. When you return that late afternoon or early evening, more than likely, the water would seem to have disappeared. It would be gone. But being the intelligent person you are, you know that this is not the case. We live in a closed, looped test-tube environment. That is, matter is neither created nor destroyed. Every molecule of matter that God created at creation is still here but may be in some other form. It oftentimes surfaces in some other elemental form. So the water does not just vanish but is converted into its gaseous state and evaporates into the atmosphere only to be used again. It is part of God's recycling mechanism. You cannot see this transformation with the naked eye, but you do see the effects of it when the water goes from noticeably wet to dry. And you can say that about anything that decomposes or breaks down to its simpler forms. Thus, as it is with water, so it is with sin; even though it appears to disappear, it does not simply vanish into thin air. Because the punishment for the sinful act is not often administered instantaneously, people more times than not, as in the case of evaporating water, often feel as if they have gotten away with it. It is gone away. Even though there may be a fleeting feeling of guilt by the perpetrator's sinful act, unless sincere repentance takes place, there is a good chance that an attempt to commit the sinful act or some other sin-laden offense again.

Without the conscientious deliberate submission to the will of God, it is not in the lowly nature of man to refrain from committing the sinful acts again automatically on his own. Remember, that we are made of the lowest particles...., dust. And it is only by God's grace and mercy that we are not consumed at the time of the offense. **"For I am the Lord, I change not therefore ye sons of Jacob are not consumed."** Mal. 3:6

He is merciful, long-suffering, and gracious. However, it needs to be made crystal clear that there is a day of reckoning approaching very rapidly. **"And the earth shall wax old like a garment."** Isa. 51:6 and His cup of indignation is filling up to the rim.

Putting this in another physical or scientific terminological perspective, it is often stated that this world is going round and round; however, because of sin, we are not just going round and round, but this old world is hurling through space at approximately 67,000 mph (miles per hour) on a one-way collision course bound straight for hell! And there is no turning it back! It is on a man-made destructive course even if God did not intervene. Be certain that if there was a beginning of which all can agree, then be also certain that there is an end approaching. Imagine, if you will, a snowball being hurled at a brick wall at about 500 mph, which is about the extent of which destruction will hit this old wicked world. **"The earth shall reel to and fro like a drunkard, and shall be removed like a cottage; and the transgression thereof shall be heavy upon it; and it shall fall and not rise again."** Isa. 24:20

It needs to be understood, deep within, that there is a penalty to be paid, and that penalty is eternal death. This is why everyone needs to get it right, right now! **"Howl ye; for the day of the Lord is at hand; it shall come as a destruction from the Almighty."** Isa. 13:6 Again, **"Alas for the day! For the day of the Lord is at hand, and as a destruction from the Almighty** it shall come." Joel 1:15 "**Blow ye the trumpet in Zion, and sound an alarm in My Holy Mountain: let all the inhabitants of the land <u>tremble</u>, for the day of the Lord cometh, for it is nigh at hand.**" Joel 2:1

No matter how large or how small the sin is, *there has to be a display of atonement for the sin by the shedding of blood.* Something has to die for the offense to God's will, not because God hates the sinner (His created being) but because He hates the sin. This is why the transgressor was required to perish for their own sins. However, there is hope; a loving God made a way for the sinner to be redeemed even though he does not deserve it. The sinner can still have life though he has sinned simply due to the magnitude of God's love. "**For God so loved the world, that He gave His only begotten Son, that whosoever believeth in Him shall not perish, but have everlasting life.**" Jn. 3:16

This is indeed the best news that could be given to a condemned sinner as is all the inhabitants of the earth. "**For all have sinned, and come short of the Glory of God.**" Rom. 3:23

It is only by the precious blood of JESUS that all those who give their heart to GOD will be redeemed from the destructive life-extracting effects and devastation of sin.

The blood of innocent animals as a sacrifice for the guilty sinner before Christ came only indicated that they believed in the true sacrifice to come. Again, when Adam and Eve sinned in the Garden of Eden, a lamb was slain for their atonement. Neither they nor anyone else since them will be saved due to the blood of an animal. Think about it. How could man, a higher order of creation, be saved by the blood of a lower order of creation—a bull, a goat, or any other animal? It does not make any sense, does it? The only thing that the blood of the animal did was to symbolize the fact that they (the sinners) believed in the true Lamb of God which was to come, which is Christ Jesus. "**For God so loved the world, that He gave His only begotten**

Son, that whosoever believeth in Him should not perish, but have ever lasting life." Jn. 3:16

Never did the Word of God make this kind of statement about any animal or any other creature for that matter. Have you noticed, hardly anyone is making sacrifices by the slaying of animals anymore? Why? Because Christ, the true Lamb of God, has come to redeem the world from sin. "But God commended His love toward us, in that, while we were yet sinners, Christ died for us." Rom. 5:8 That is, He died for you and me.

It also needs to be pointed out that the angels who were made a little higher than man could not have made atonement for man's sins either. Even though, unlike the animals, the angels are higher forms and stand in the presence of God, but their blood just simply could not suffice. "For unto which of the angels said He at any time, thou art My Son, this day have I begotten thee?" Heb. 1:5

Angels, men, and animals are created beings and subjected to the same laws of GOD as are all creatures of the universe. Some of the angels wanted to offer themselves but could not. It had to be God himself in the form of Jesus Christ the Son. "I and My Father are one." John 10:30

What measure of love is demonstrated here? Only His blood that is above the law and never broken the law could be an effective atonement for those sins of created beings under the law. It also needs to be noted that He did not have to do it. He could have simply wiped the slate clean and made a whole new world if He wanted to. But He did not, and while going through your test-tube experience, you must determine whether or not you will continue to live a life of sin to satisfy your own will or subject yourself to the will of the Almighty God who made you in His image.

Time is in fact, as well as indeed, running out! This world cannot forever keep going the way it has always been going. "And the earth shall wax old like a garment," Isa. 51:6

Common sense should reveal that the end is approaching even if the word or the will of God is unknown. **"For we know that the whole creation groaneth and travaileth in pain together until now."** Rom. 8:22

Man cannot continue to rape and plunder the earth and not put one thing back! We know that the end is very near, and it is high time that each of us get it right with our Heavenly Father and His Son Christ Jesus today. **"And when these things begin to come to pass, then look up, and lift up your heads; for your redemption draweth nigh."** Lk 21:28

It is also important to note that your test tube is your environment. Where you live, work, and play is the observation medium by which you are being observed. It is the theater or stage of action where you are being observed and/or tested. Nowhere else could Adam and Eve have been tested other than at the tree of knowledge of good and evil in the garden of Eden.

As a child psychologist may observe and record the behavior of children on a play yard, so are your actions being observed and recorded on the stage of life both by good and by dark spiritual powers that you may or may not be aware of. For example, if you have been leading a lifestyle devoid of Christ and mostly, if not entirely concerning self, and you purpose at some point in your life that you have had enough of this world-seeking self-gratification, and you decide to take your stand on the side of righteousness. That is to take a firmer stand for Christ, to increase your spirituality, and to become more like Jesus; do you think for one moment that the enemies of righteousness are going to sit back and twiddle their thumbs while you go waltzing into heaven? Absolutely not! As a matter of fact, you will be tried by the powers that be to see if your heart is sincerely given over to your new profession because anything can be uttered with the lips and the heart be given over to other desires. **"These people draweth nigh [near] unto me with their mouth, and honoureth me with their lips; but their heart is far from me. But in vain they do worship me, teaching for doctrines the commandments of men."** Matt. 15:8, 9

It is holistically necessary that the heart be given over entirely to God in order for the redemption that He has set in place for us to work for us. The trying of your faith is not for your demise but for your refinement and correction of character. In other words, God loves you and will fashion you into a better person with stronger faith in the end if the trials are endured. As gold is tried in the fire, so shall your faith be established.

Touching on this test-tube real-life experience, it can actually be placed in a simple mathematical equation:

(**JESUS** [The Word of God] **+ SINFUL MAN** [US] **= THE PLAN OF SALVATION**). In mathematics, you may have an equation with variables and fixed numbers. For example, in a simple algebraic equation $2x + 1 = 9$, all factors in this simple equation is fixed except the x, which is in this case a variable. In this simple linear expression x could be 4 or the square root of 16, or 2 square for that matter. Whichever number used, x is a variable. Now concerning the above equation, **Jesus (the Word of God) plus sinful man(us) equal the plan of salvation.** The Word of God (Jesus) and the plan of salvation are both fixed. **"Every good gift and every perfect gift is from above and cometh down from the Father of lights, with whom there is no variableness, neither shadow of turning."** James 1:17 There is no variableness with God. He is what He is. He, His Word, and His Spirit are and always will be permanent fixtures they do not alter or change. **"And God said unto Moses, 'I AM THAT I AM;' and He said, 'Thus shalt you say unto the children of Israel, I AM hath sent me unto you.'"** Ex. 3:14 This is what He told Moses to tell them when asked what His name was.

God nor the plan of salvation **cannot** and **will not** change. The plan of salvation exists only because of sin. If sin had never entered the world, all factors would have then been fixed forever and the equation may have been something like **Jesus + Created beings = Eternity.** There would have been no need to implement the plan of salvation, and we probably would not have known about the plan or it may have been part of our study throughout the ceaseless ages of eternity. In any case, the only variable in the entire equation now is sinful man. And guess what; man invariably needs to change! If we intend to inherit all the promises that are given to us by our Heavenly Father, then we need to take on His character and start acting and reacting like His children. In other words, behaving as Christ would! From birth, there is a natural tendency to go astray. This is why the Lord is always saying things like, **"Turn O backsliding children, saith the Lord."** Jer. 3:14 and **"Return unto me, and I will return unto you, saith the Lord of hosts."** Mal. 3:7

He is always pleading for us to come to or return to Him. If there is a need to alter your course and come to the Lord, then evidently somewhere in times past you have never come to Him or you have been with Him and changed for the worse. There is the possibility that you started to go in the wrong direction. Going against God's will simply mean sin has entered into your life. Adam and Eve did it when they ate from the forbidden tree of knowledge of good and evil. And there is no record of what sins they may have committed after the initial sin of eating from the tree. The Bible does not list every sin that every person in the Bible ever committed, but we do know that after the first parents ate the forbidden fruit, the preplanned plan of salvation was called into action. The plan of salvation is now implemented and fixed. It cannot be changed nor altered. **"And all that dwell upon the earth shall worship Him, whose names are not written in the book of life of the Lamb slain from the foundation of the world."** Rev. 13:8 From the foundation of the world, the redemptive plan of salvation was already in place and implemented by the birth, death, and resurrection of the Messiah.

The solution to the problem of overcoming sin and self is not an easy task due to the factor of resistance to the change. First, there must be a realization that you are primarily serving self and not God. The chains that bind and keep us in bondage to sin are not so easily broken. As a matter of fact, it is impossible to break and completely get rid of the chains that bind us on our own. Any attempt to clean up self is only behavior modification and without Christ may work for a while, but more often than not, old self almost always creeps back in. The old man (self) without Christ rises up again and again and again. Only through Christ can true and permanent reformation take place with a noticeable difference in the life of the sinner. **"Create in me a clean heart, o God, and renew a right Spirit within me."** Ps. 51:10 and **"Come unto me, all ye that labor and are heavy laden, and I will give you rest. Take my yoke upon you, *and learn of Me*; for I am meek and lowly in heart: and ye shall find rest unto your souls."** Matt. 11:28, 29

So the first step for everyone, whether a person just beginning to seek Christ or an old believer who do honor Him with their lips but their heart is not truly with Him, need to recognize that there is a problem with uplifting self and self-gratification. Recognition for change is step number one! With a prayerful subdued heart, confess it all and give it all to Christ Jesus.

After recognizing the spiritual need for the Savior and a closer walk with Him, come to Him, then after you take His yoke upon you, the next criteria is *to learn of Me*, JESUS says. **"If we say that we have no sin, we deceive ourselves, and the truth is not in us. If we confess our sins, He is faithful and just to forgive us our sins, and to cleanse us from <u>all</u> unrighteousness."** 1 Jn. 1:8, 9

There are also times when one Christian has a lengthier Christian walk than another. The person who claims to have been in the faith longer may naturally think that they have it more together than the person who is new to the faith. After all, some have been in the faith twenty, thirty, forty, fifty or more years, and say things like "Who are they to tell me anything about the Christian walk of faith? They've only been in this thing for a short while." The person who thinks this way need to reconsider their theological position and reevaluate themselves in more cases than not. If it is really given some thought, the people who claim to have been walking the longest with Christ may be the very ones who need to do the most vigorous self-evaluations. The word of God says, **"Seeing ye are dull of hearing. For when for the time ye ought to be teachers, ye have need that one teach <u>you</u> again, which be the** first oracles of God; and are become such as have need of milk, and not of strong meat." Heb. 5:11 and 12 Jesus also admonishes us to be cold or hot because if we are lukewarm, He will spit us out of His mouth. A cold person is one who does not know Him, and a hot person may very well be that on-fire new believer that is being pushed aside. But the worst ones are those lukewarm Christians who claim to know Christ but are really in the way of spiritual growth for God's church and are hated by God the most. Therefore, He will spit them out of His mouth as proclaimed in the Book of Revelation. **"So then because you are lukewarm, and neither cold nor hot, I will spue you out of My mouth."** Rev. 3:16 **In other words if you are a lukewarm Christian your very name would be distasteful to God.**

One of the most profound errors a person who think they are Christian can make, because they think they have so much knowledge of the Bible or to have been sitting on a church pew for more years than someone else, that they think they have the Spirit of God. That is a self-inflicted hard-to-cure wound. They have in essence placed a spiritual bullet into their own heart. And they also think that by knowledge alone, it will gain them accommodations to a first-class seat on the heaven-bound chariot. Constant recognition needs to be assessed by the believer because you can be, **"Ever learning, and never able to come to the full knowledge of the truth."** 2 Tim. 3:7

Therefore you can be going through your reaction experience in a comfort zone. Being tested without going through the fire! Sitting on a church pew and believing everything is all right when in fact you can be wretched, poor, blind, miserable, naked, and bound straight for hell!

To become complacent in sin or lukewarm is one of the biggest hurdles one may have to overcome because it may be thought that everything is all right. When in all actuality, it is not. **"I know thy works, that thou are neither cold nor hot: I would thou wert cold or hot. So then because thou art lukewarm,"** [complacent] **"I will spue thee out of my mouth. Because thou sayest, I am rich, and increased with goods, and have need** of nothing; and knowest not that thou art wretched, and miserable, and poor, and blind, and naked." Rev. 3:15–17 The Lord counsels us to look to Him and turn from our sins because sin will mess you up and destroy you if you let it!

Another thing to remember about sin is that it is like a virus. As a viral infection will attempt to take over or consume the entire host organism that it infects, so it is with sin. Also, as viral infections may become worse and more difficult to treat because of mutations, so it is with sin. When one sin is committed, it may cause you (the host) to produce other unnoticeable bad habits until you are consumed in your iniquities. Once sin has been committed, the second time around does not seem as bad. In other words, it becomes easier to commit the sinful act with the very next temptation. So it is with the third, the fourth, and so on, until finally sin has totally consumed the individual and they are found on skid row, death row, or the morgue, to name a few places. **"And that they may recover themselves out of the snare of the devil, who are taken captive by him at his will."** 2 Tim. 2:26

Consider this: a person who drinks may get lured into smoking marijuana for the first time. If the act was enjoyed, not only does the second time for smoking becomes less obstructive, but the chances of graduating to harder and more dangerous drugs become less challenging. They are easier to do. Before you know it, the person, who at first had a rather difficult time getting to take the first hit off of a joint, is now on skid row with a debilitating habit of crack cocaine or heroin or both and wondering, "How in the world did I get here?" Okay, let us not just batter the substance abusers; this same analogy can be applied concerning any sin: adultery, fornication, lying, stealing, covetousness, and/or any sin. Sin will mess you up! And it does not care what color, race, or gender you are. Sin is not prejudiced. Satan wants all to be hell bound and he is not race particular. Sin does not care how much education you have or how smart you may think you are. It does not care what your economic status is or which level you are on with the corporation.

Eventually sin *will* destroy you. And it comes after you like a hound after a rabbit. On its own, it does not raise up off of you! It keeps coming and is in fact all around you! That is why it is very important for the child of GOD to stay linked up with JESUS. He is the only way to overcome sin and for the sinner to be kept from sinning. Sanctification is a lifelong process! There is absolutely no way for you to overcome sin in your own strength. You will lose more times than not when trying to fight it alone. Only in JESUS can the sinner truly overcome. **"If we confess our sins, He is faithful and just to forgive us our sins, and to cleanse us from all unrighteousness."** 1 Jn. 1:9

So the biblical answer to the question, "What is sin?" is simply **"Sin is the transgression of the law."** 1 Jn. 3:4 It is also very important that this God-given definition is understood and always remembered.

Now the question begs itself: Where did sin come from? Some believe it came from Adam and Eve in the Garden of Eden. This is a mistake and a deception. Sin began with Lucifer in heaven. Wait a minute, there was "war in heaven," do you mean there was *sin* there too? Many people (including some theologians) also believe that God made Satan. He did not. God made Lucifer. Lucifer decided to transgress against God and therefore sinned and over the process of time while the sin matriculated, he evolved into Satan with other names and titles of devil, deceiver, serpent, dragon, etc. Lucifer at first created did not have any of these titles. **"How art thou fallen from heaven, O Lucifer, son of the morning! How art thou cut down to the ground, which didst weaken the nations! For thou hast said in thine heart, I will ascend into heaven, I will exalt my throne above the stars of God: I will sit also upon the mount of the congregation, in the sides of the north: I will ascend above the heights of the clouds; I will be like the Most High."** Isa. 14:12–14

Comparing the king of Tyrus to Lucifer, God describes as this: **"Thus saith the Lord God, 'Thou sealest up the sum, full of wisdom, and perfect in beauty. Thou hast been in Eden the garden of God; every precious** stone was thy covering, the sardius, topaz, and the diamond, the beryl, the onyx, and the jasper, the sapphire, the emerald, and the carbuncle, and gold: the workmanship of thy tabrets and of thy pipes was prepared in thee in the day that thou wast created. Thou art the anointed cherub that covereth; and *I have set thee so*: thou wast upon the holy mountain of God,: thou hast walked up and down in the midst of the stones of fire. Thou wast perfect in thy ways from the day that thou wast *created*, <u>till iniquity was, found in thee</u>.'" Ezek. 28:11-15

As can be plainly seen, God made Lucifer the cherub that covers. He made him a very beautiful anointed cherub and perfect in his ways until iniquity or sin was found in him. It was at this time "Till iniquity was found in him" that he became the enemy of God and was cast down with a name change. **"And there was war in heaven: Michael and his angels fought against the dragon; and the dragon fought and his angels, and prevailed not; neither was their place found any more in heaven. And the great dragon was cast out, that old serpent, called the devil and satan, which deceiveth the whole world: he was cast out into the earth and his angels were cast out with him."** Rev. 12:7-9 Based on these biblical facts, it is readily seen and should be clear that God did not create Satan but Lucifer the anointed cherub that covereth. It was only by Lucifer's transgressions that he became Satan, the dragon, the devil, etc.

(With deception, eloquence, and skill, Satan is still perpetuating sin and error here on earth as a musical conductor leads a harmonic symphony.)

Even though God clearly revealed to us where sin comes from and with whom it originated, it is not holistically given to us how it started. Think about it, as described above in the quote by Ezekiel, God could not have made Lucifer any better than if He had recreated Himself! God said that He made Lucifer very beautiful, very powerful, and perfect in all his ways till iniquity was found in him. Here is arguably the second most powerful agent in the entire universe. He was the first of created beings, therefore making him second only to God who is of course a non-created being. What on earth or in heaven could have possessed Lucifer to go against his maker, the Creator? The Bible calls it a mystery. Sin began in a mystical sort of way. The Bible's only emphasis placed on the origin of sin is when it mentions, "Till iniquity was found in thee." But the apostle Paul, however, does let us know that sin is a mystery when he was addressing the Thessalonians, **"For the mystery of iniquity doth already work:"** 2 Thess. 2:7 While the questions of who, when, and why sin came about was given to us, at this present time, the answer to the question as to how sin came about is simply given to us that it is a mystery. Though sin is a mystery and really should have never surfaced in God's perfectly created universe, it did. And though at present we cannot fully ascertain as to how the initial thought of Lucifer wanting to supersede and dethrone God his maker, we do know that he did. The why is explained as he wanted to dethrone God by exalting himself because of his beauty and corrupted his wisdom by reason of his brightness. We can, at this time, only speculate as to how this sinful act crept up in Lucifer's heart to do what he did until there becomes an end of sin and we are able to confirm our study from the testaments of heaven as we reign with Christ our Savior.

your adynamy

heaven, and did

as He was born, what

your child as soon

though so

THE CHALLENGE

Again, the earth in general is the test tube for man. However, your environment or the part of the vineyard where you interact with others (that is where you live, work, and play) is your life's test tube or as would be said in chemistry, your reaction medium. It is the stage of life where you are being observed by the spiritual powers of both good and evil.

The first test-tube experience that we are aware of originated in heaven. Fact is that God never changes, **"I am the Lord, I change not, therefore you sons of Jacob are not consumed."** Mal. 3:6 Based on this premise, we can infer that a similar testing or trial situation took place in heaven as it did down here on earth. As noted in the previous chapter, sin originated in heaven by that arch deceiver Lucifer who ultimately became Satan after the mystery of sin developed in him by transgressing the express will of God. That is in trespassing GOD's law and/or His commandments.

Because Lucifer was a covering cherub in heaven, he held a high command. Now there may or may not be such a thing as an angel's Bible, but because the Lord changes not, it can be deduced that Lucifer, along with all the other angels, were told to worship and obey Jesus the Son of God as was man here on earth. **"Thy kingdom come, Thy will be done in earth, as it is in heaven."** Matt. 6:10

Jesus, operating at that time under the name of Michael, whom Lucifer thought, was also a created being. This may have well been his test as well as the test of the entire heavenly host. It is possible that all of heaven complied for a while. Then something strange begins to happen. The mystery of iniquity begins to take form. As it did in Ancient Israel's day, as it did in the early church's day, and as it has done in the latter church of God today! Lucifer thought that he was the high command. Pride had set in, and there was no turning back. **"Pride goeth before destruction, and a haughty spirit before a fall."** Prov. 16:18

The possibility exists that Lucifer may have said something on this wise, "Who is this Jesus that I in all my glory should bow down to worship Him?" Therefore the scriptures are fulfilled in saying, **"Thou art the anointed cherub that covereth; and I have set thee so; thou wast upon the Holy Mountain of GOD; thou hast walked up and down in the midst of the stones of fire. Thou was perfect in thy ways from the day that thou wast** *created*, **till** <u>iniquity</u> **was found in thee."** Ezek. 28:14, 15

Needless to say, Lucifer failed the test. Lucifer had a highly-respectable position. He stood in the very presence of Almighty GOD, but that was not enough for him. He wanted more. Not only did he not want to worship GOD, but also he wanted to exalt himself above GOD and attempt to actually dethrone and replace our Lord and Savior Jesus Christ. This is why sin was manifested. **"Who opposeth and exalteth himself above all that is called GOD, or that is worshipped; so that he as God sitteth in the temple of God, showing himself that he is GOD."** 2 Thess. 2:4

Lucifer first entertained the thought of rebellion. He wanted to be like the most high. **"How art thou fallen from heaven, O Lucifer, son of the morning! How art thou cut down to the ground, which didst weaken the nations! For thou hast said in thine heart, I will ascend into heaven, I will exalt my throne above the stars of God: I will sit also upon the mount of the sides of the congregation, in the sides of the north: I will ascend above the heights of the clouds; I will be like the Most High."** Isa. 14:12–14

After entertaining those rebellious thoughts, instead of putting the destructive thoughts behind him and moving on to do what he was created to do, his focus begin to escalate into open rebellion. He has passed the point of no return, and now the birth of sin within the universe has broken forth from the womb of transgression. Lucifer has now transformed into Satan. He is no longer this highly exalted cherub that covereth! He now begins walking through the heavenly throngs spreading discord. **"Frowardness is in his heart, he deviseth mischief continually, he soweth discord."** Prov. 6:14

After gaining the allegiance of approximately a third of the heavenly host by deception and lies, Satan thought that he would attack the government of GOD with his newly created army of rebellious angels.

A point to note here is that these angels had every opportunity to turn back and return their allegiance back to Creator GOD. It has been mentioned by some that about half were swayed to follow the deceptions at the first but upon further consideration, some of them decided not to and returned to their ranks with the good angels. The result was thirty-three and one-third percent of the heavenly throng was eventually given over to the hellish lies and deceptions of Satan. **"And there appeared another wonder in heaven; and behold a great red dragon, having seven heads and then horns, and seven crowns upon his heads. And his tail drew the third part of the stars of heaven, and did cast them to the earth."** Rev.12:3 and 4 This is how it is known that one third of the angels fell with the evil one that they followed. And his tail drew the third part of the stars of heaven, and did cast them to the earth.

Most know that if GOD wanted to, He could have destroyed the entire rebellious throng, but because all of heaven had heard these false accusations, if GOD had destroyed them right there on the spot, then all the universe would have served God out of fear as opposed to love. And we also know that GOD is a God of love. **"For God so loved the world that He gave His only begotten Son that whosoever believeth in Him should not perish, but have everlasting life."** Jn. 3:16 Also, in addition to the above statement, there may have been another opportunity for sin to arise a second time. However,

GOD is a GOD of *love*, and in His infinite wisdom, He decided to let this thing called sin play itself out in order that the entire universe and un-fallen beings could see the arch deceiver, the creator of sin in his true form as well as the devastation and anguish sin can cause.

His lying, deceptive, and conniving ways had to be exposed to the fullest. So GOD Himself allowed war to break out in heaven when opposition against His own authority presented itself, that over time His true love would be manifested without any doubt. **"And there was war in heaven: Michael [Jesus] and His angels fought against the dragon [satan]; and the dragon fought and his angels, And prevailed not; neither was their place found any more in heaven."** Rev. 12:7 and 8

Why is not their place found any more in heaven? Where did they go? Did this once-powerful angel (the dragon) and all the fallen angels under him go off on some distant planet in the far reaches of the universe? Did they get zapped into nothingness? The answer to both questions is no, absolutely not! Make no mistake; they are all right here on planet Earth! **"Therefore rejoice ye heavens, and ye that dwell in them. <u>Woe</u> to the inhabiters of the earth and of the sea! For the devil is come down unto you, having great wrath, because he knoweth that he hath but a short time."** Rev. 12:12

Therefore, my friends, be it known that the enemy of all righteousness is not off on some distant planet warring against other inhabitants of the universe but has come down unto all the inhabitants of this planet called Earth. We are at war! **"And it was given unto him to make war with the saints, and to overcome them: and power was given him over all kindreds, and tongues, and nations."** Rev. 13:7

And keep in mind, the battlefront is not way off on some distant planet or shore, but spiritual warfare is what each of us is engaged in each day of our lives. The battlefield is most often within the confines of the individual's mind. **"From whence come wars and fightings among you? Come they not hence, even of your lusts that war in your members?"** James 4:1 The choices you make ultimately determine which side you are on and whether or not you have gotten the victory over sin through Christ Jesus our Lord. This is one of the reasons why GOD and all the un-fallen inhabitants of the universe take such a special interest in this little old planet called Earth. They all observe planet Earth to see if there is anyone down here in this sin-infested test tube that can keep GOD's way and be saved.

Strange and untrue accusations were made against the sovereignty of the universe in heaven by the father of lies. Therefore, a test-tube situation was formed on earth to see if a lower created being, lower than the angels, could keep God's commandments and do His will from a perspective of love without being forced to do so. You see, as far as we know, there were only two sets of moral beings created that are associated with this planet. There may very well be others in the universe but we are not privileged with that information. However, what is needed for our learning and our salvation to have a closer walk with the Lord was given to us. **"For whatsoever things were written aforetime were written for our learning, that we through patience and comfort of the scriptures might have hope."** Rom. 15:4

Now a horse, a dog, or a giraffe cannot make moral decisions, reason, or naturally follow logical deductions. Unlike plant life, animals are animated, created beings. That is, they can conscientiously move around if they want to. They are, for the most part, preprogrammed, but they can, however, be trained to do things that they normally would not do. For instance, a dog can be trained to stay or to roll over and play dead at the master's command. These are things that the animal probably would not do under normal circumstances. They exist solely on instinctual behavior. They were created a little higher than the plants, or to phrase it, in a way similar to how we are related to angels. As we were made a little lower than the angels, it can be stated that the plants were made a little lower than the animals because they too are alive and living.

Plants have life and are made from compositions of the earth but are not, for the most part, animated. However, unlike humans who are also animated, animals cannot make moral decisions. They were made a little lower than humans. Humans, as well as angels, are capable of making moral decisions and the ability to follow logical deductive reasoning; angels have the ability to exist and interact within the spiritual realm as well as the physical world. Man too can interact with the spiritual world but not of the order as angels do. Man was made a little lower than the angels. **"What is man, that Thou art mindful of him? And the son of man, that Thou visitest him? For Thou hast made him a little lower than the angels, and hast crowned him with glory and honour."** Ps 8:4 and 5

Therefore, angels are of a higher order. **"But we see Jesus, who was made a little lower than the angels for the suffering of death, crowned with glory and honour; that He by the grace of God should taste death for every man."** Heb. 2:9

Angels can transcend down into the physical world and be seen of men if there is a need for them to. Humans were made a little lower than the angels, but all the angels, no matter how high their position, are created beings and therefore lower than GOD, their creator. Angels though, they exist in the spiritual world; they are capable of making choices, and like some humans, they do not always make the best ones. As seen with the third of angels that were thrown out of heaven how they made some very poor moral decisions and fail due to the whims of the arch deceiver. On a day-to-day basis, man also is following the same pathway and like it or not, the final destination is death in a lake burning with fire and brimstone. **"Then when lust hath conceived, it bringeth forth sin: and sin, when it is finished bringeth forth death."** James 1:15

Whenever a personal trial becomes eminent, the individual is placed within a character test-tube observational arena at that precise point in time, and there is a true heavenly recording made on the outcome. Realized or not, an accurate recording is being kept on all inhabitants of the test tube. Every little lie, every little theft, every coveted thought, every sin whether big or small is noted. This is why it is important not to give in to sin and relent to say things like, "Oh well, I can't give this lustful habit up, so I might as well just keep on doing it." "Jesus will forgive me any way," some may proclaim. This is a dangerous submission to sin and a hardening of heart to the impress of the Holy Spirit. No matter how good it feels, looks, or tastes, it is sin and should be eliminated from the Christian's walk and talk. **"Wherefore seeing we are also compassed about with so great a cloud of witnesses, let us lay aside every weight, and the sin which doeth so easily beset us,"** Heb. 12:1 Giving in to habitual lying or gambling is no less sin than a thief that finds it difficult to give up stealing.

Sin is manifested in our lives much the same way as it started with Lucifer. First, the thought is conceived within our psyche in some shape, form, or fashion. Often, a temptation is summoned before you. Sin begins in the lustful heart (the mind). **"What shall we say then? Is the Law sin? God forbid. Nay, I had not known sin, but by the Law: for I had not known lust, except the law had said, 'Thou shalt not covet.'"** Rom. 7:7

Every action that takes place in our lives must pass through the mind whether it is a conscious or unconscious thought process. It is almost impossible to do anything without it first being registered in the brain. You can insist that "The devil made me do it," but you had to make the choice to do it! The devil can only tempt you to sin; he cannot make you sin. It is a choice made by the sinful mind.

The sinful thought enters the mind and instead of immediately dismissing the idea, by focusing on Jesus, the mistake is often made of flirting with the sinful thought. Like Eve, flirting with the idea that the fruit from the tree of good and evil was pleasant to the eyes and able to make one wise, she, by entertaining the thought, resigned to actually carrying out the sinful act as did Lucifer in heaven. **"Then when lust is conceived, it bringeth forth sin; and sin, when it is finished, bringeth forth death."** James 1:15

No matter how you slice it, the end result of sin is death. It does not matter how appealing it might be or how sweet, delicious, and entertaining it may be to the senses; the end result of sin is always death. Because of sin, the transgressor is required to die but because of the love and grace of God, Christ died in behalf of all repentant sinners. Unrepentant sinners with much dismay must die for their own sins. **"The wages of sin is death; but the gift of God is eternal life through Jesus Christ our Lord."** Rom. 6:23 Therefore, the commission and challenge is to follow righteousness in Christ and sin will flee from you. **"Submit yourselfs therefore unto God. Resist the devil, and he will flee from you." Jam.4:7** And also, **"Be ye therefore perfect, even as your Father which is in heaven is perfect."** Matt. 5:48

ANCIENT ISRAEL

GOD, in His supreme wisdom and infinite love, provided an avenue by which man could be saved despite man's sinful nature. Man did not deserve to be saved; it was only by GOD's grace and His unfaltering love that we have this great opportunity to dwell with GOD and to live with CHRIST throughout the ceaseless ages of eternity. It should be perfectly clear that this is why man was made. God loves every one of us so much that He wants all who have ever lived to forever live with HIM. But if a person, a church, or a nation does not make it in, it is not because God did not want them too. It boils down to a matter of choice. God will not force anyone to serve Him but desires that all do. He wants very much to be our God and Father. **"Have I any pleasure at all that the wicked should die?" Saith the LORD GOD, "and not that he should return from his ways, and live?"** Ezek. 18:23

Because of God's love for us and His hatred of sin, the LORD necessitated a mechanism by which He could salvage man, whom He loved so dearly. The REDEEMER (the catalyst by which every man would be enhanced or restricted while going through their test-tube experiences) had to come in the form of flesh as man himself did. **"Wherefore when He cometh into the world, He saith, Sacrifice and offering thou wouldest not, but a body Thou hast prepared me."** Heb. 10:5

Because man had the ability to choose and because of the possibility of him making the incorrect choice as he did, going against God's original plan, a plan had already been devised by which *all* men could be saved. This divine plan was established before sin ever surfaced on earth. **"And all that dwell upon the earth shall worship Him, whose names are not written in the book of life of the Lamb slain from the foundation of the world."** Rev. 13:8

Because it was man who needed to be redeemed, then GOD had to come as a man in the flesh. And because GOD had to come as a man, then He had to have a human lineage and a medium (a fleshly body) by which to manifest Himself (interject Himself) into this lost world of sin as the true sacrifice. In other words, He had to have a bloodline.

Remember that man was made from dust and after sin came into a perfect world; it was man's natural tendency to moralistically spiral downward and follow after his own inclinations as opposed to following GOD's. **"And God saw that the wickedness of man was great in the earth, and that <u>every</u> imagination of the thoughts of his heart was only evil continually."** Gen. 6:5

At the first destruction of the world, there were only eight people who went into GOD's ark of safety: Noah, the messenger of God, his three sons Japheth, Shem, and Ham, and each of their wives for a total of eight people. Noah was selected because he walked with GOD and obeyed His voice. **"But Noah found grace in the eyes of the Lord. Noah was a just man and perfect in his generations and Noah walked with God."** Gen. 6:8 and 9

Two things should be noted here. One, grace has always existed with GOD. Unlike some may think, grace did not suddenly surface in New Testament times; it existed also in the old. Two, Noah was "perfect in his generations." "Noah found grace in the eyes of the LORD and he also was perfect in his generations," the Bible says. Striving daily for the light of a perfect walk with the Redeemer in this dark world should be the order of the day for every Christian. The Redeemer Himself says, **"Be ye therefore perfect, even as your Father who is in heaven is perfect."** Matt. 5:48

There had to have been other tests not mentioned in the sacred texts that Noah had to endure because it was mentioned that he was a just man and perfect in the sight of GOD. In order to be found perfect, there has to be trails, tribulations, and temptations to overcome. Noah evidently passed the tests. **"These [are] the generations of Noah: Noah was a just man [and] perfect in his generations, [and] Noah walked with God."** Gen. 6:9

It is revealed, however, the most important test of Noah's life. The one where he was told by GOD that a hard rain was coming and for him to build the most massive boat ever to be built at that time on the topside of the earth. It was to be built on dry land when it had never, up until that time, before rained. Noah was to construct an ark. GOD gave him the dimensions and materials to be used. And he was instructed to preach until it was finished; for one hundred and twenty years, Noah proclaimed the revelation of the ensuing water storm to an apostate and rebellious world. Noah passed the test with flying colors. Though ridiculed, mocked, and looked down upon by the surrounding peoples of the earth, he did exactly as he was instructed and by doing so, he, along with his family, were saved by God from foretold destruction. We are in the same boat today! There is a spiritual ark being constructed right now, and all who plan to be saved need to be getting on board. Not getting ready to get on board but to be getting on board. Right now is the time to climb aboard God's ark of safety in Christ Jesus! **"Behold, I stand at the door, and knock: if any man hear My voice, and open the door, I will come in to him, and will sup with him, and he with me."** Rev. 3:20

The human element of GOD's plan of salvation (the Redeemer) had to come by way of one of Noah's three sons because they were the only ones saved from the destroyed life on the planet. Noah's second born son Shem's blood line was selected by God to usher in The Messiah and complete the plan of salvation. It stands to reason that God, being a God of order and one who never changes, has almost always used a son not of the firstborn position of the family. If you consider since the beginning of time, it was Abel and Seth as opposed to the firstborn Cain, Isaac as opposed to Ishmael, Jacob over Esau, Moses before the firstborn Aaron, Judah and Joseph as opposed to Reuben, and the list goes on and on whereby the providence of GOD, the firstborn was hardly ever used for his major purposes. King David was the last son of Jesse, his father. And King Solomon was not the firstborn of King David, his father. Even with Christ Jesus, the second Adam was utilized as our Redeemer as opposed to the first Adam that fail. **"And so it is written, 'The first man Adam was made a living soul; the last Adam was made a quickening Spirit.'"** 1 Cor. 15:45

So then, it should come as no surprise for God to have selected the line from Shem, the second born middle child of Noah, for the Messiah to manifest Himself.

The story is well-known of how after the flood, Noah planted a vineyard and became drunk with the wine produced from it. The story informs how Noah was asleep within his tent when his youngest son Ham came in and saw his father's nakedness. After seeing it, like some people today, he had to go and tell it. Ham revealed what he had seen to his two brothers, Japheth and Shem. Unlike Ham, these two decided to place a blanket over their shoulders while going in backward to avert seeing their father's nakedness and to cover him in the process. The scriptures does not specify which one of Noah's two sons, Shem or Japheth, came up with the idea to go in backward with the garment over their shoulders to cover their father's nakedness. It is of necessity to note and deduce that because of the order, magnitude, and extent of the blessings, Noah bestowed upon his sons that there is a good possibility Japheth the firstborn was indeed the one who came up with the idea to go in backward with the covering to cover their father's nakedness, and Shem agreed.

This premise is based upon the cursing and the blessings that Noah bestowed upon each of his three sons, with Ham receiving what is perceived to be the worst and Japheth the more preferable blessing. Upon awakening, Noah was terribly upset with his youngest son Ham and pleased with what his older two sons had done and begins to deal with them accordingly with cursing and blessings. **"And Noah awoke from his wine, and knew what** his younger son had done unto him. And he said, 'Cursed be Canaan; a servant of servants shall he be unto his brethren.' And he said, 'Blessed be the LORD God of Shem; and Canaan shall be his servant.' God shall enlarge Japheth, and he shall dwell in the tents of Shem, and Canaan shall be his servant." Gen. 9:24–27

If given some thought concerning the blessing and curse pronounced on each son back then, they have in fact as well as indeed came to pass and has been fulfilled as can be observed in this present day.

Japheth's lineage has become enlarged throughout the earth. They have encompassed the whole Earth and inhabited and controlled almost every land they have so desired. But even with that, the lineage of the Messiah was to promulgate through was not to be in Noah's firstborn. And also remember that Noah passed away without really knowing which line of his three sons God would select to accomplish his mission. He did state, however, that Japheth would dwell in the tents of Shem indicating that somehow Shem would provide a form of shelter for his older brother. Today we know that it was Shem's lineage God used for the purpose of the blessed Redeemer. **"And he said, 'Blessed be the LORD GOD of Shem, and Canaan shall be his servant.'"** Gen. 9:26, but Japheth was to dwell in the tents of Shem. In other words, Japheth can be saved by fellowshipping or tabernacling with Shem.

Also, it would be of benefit to note that God did not select the line of Shem because he was the most knowledgeable or the most handsome or the greater in number or anything of that worldly sort. It was of a spiritual sort and simply because of the faith of Abraham that the Hebrew people were selected. And by God's providence, they were from the lineage of Shem, Noah's second born! **"The LORD did not set His love upon you, nor choose you, because you were more in number than any people; for you were the fewest of all people."** Deut. 7:7 **"Because that Abraham obeyed My voice, and kept My Charge, My commandments, My statutes, and My laws."** Gen. 26:5

Terah was a descendant of Shem and the father of Abram. Abram, by faith, followed GOD as did Noah in his day. The families of the earth had been separated because of their attempt to build a tower into the heavens. Like times of today, most men on the earth at that time were trying to accomplish things they had no business pursuing. First, their thoughts were to attempt to reside in the heavens where GOD's temple was. They wanted to ascend into the heavens and possibly set up their kingdom on the sides of the north. Sounds familiar? **"For thou hast said in thine heart, I will ascend into heaven; I will exalt my throne above the stars of God: I will sit also upon the mount of the congregation, in the sides of the north. I will ascend above the heights of the clouds; I will be like the Most High"** Isa. 14:13 and 14

They were also in defiance of GOD by building the tower trying to prevent being overtaken by a flood should one were to come a second time. They were doing this even though GOD had promised that He would not again destroy the earth by water. **"And it shall come to pass, when I bring a cloud over the earth, that the bow shall be seen in the cloud: And I will remember My covenant, which is between Me and you and of every living creature of all flesh; and the waters shall no more become a flood to destroy all flesh."** Gen. 9:14 and 15

Because of their corruptions, God confounded their language to confuse them and to therefore retard or hinder their further construction of the tower. It was then that the people left off from building the tower and migrated to different corners of the earth based on their ability to understand one another. Hence you have the various races, nations, and people speaking many different languages grouped in diverse places of the earth. **"So the LORD scattered them abroad from thence upon the face of all the earth: and they left off building the city. Therefore is the name of it called Babel; because the LORD did there confound the language of all the earth: and from there did the LORD scatter them abroad upon the face of all the earth."** Gen. 11:8 and 9

They, the men of the earth, begin to entertain other gods and devote their worship and allegiance to other entities rather than to the true GOD, the creator of the universe. They begin to form gods with their own hands and worship them. (Take note, the same things are going on today.) **"The smith with the tongs both worketh in the coals, and fashioneth it with hammers, and worketh it with the strength of his arms: yea, he is hungry, and his strength faileth: he drinketh no water, and is faint. The carpenter stretcheth out his rule; he market it out with a line; he fitteth it with planes, and he marketh it out with the compass, and maketh it after the figure of a man, according to the beauty of a man; that it may remain in the house. He heweth him down cedars, and taketh the cypress and the oak, which he strengtheneth for himself among the trees of the forest: he planteth an ash, and the rain doth nourish it. Then shall it be for a man to burn: for he will take thereof, and warm himself; yea he kindleth it, and baketh bread; yea, he maketh a god, and worshippeth it; he maketh it a graven image, and falleth down thereto. He burneth part thereof in the fire; with part thereof he eateth flesh; he roasteth roast, and is satisfied: yea, he warmeth himself, and saith, 'Deliver me; for thou art my god.' They have not known nor understood: for he hath shut their eyes, that they cannot see; and their hearts, that they cannot understand."** Isa. 44:12–18

Men were making and worshipping their own gods, but there was a man by the name of Abram who by faith followed the true GOD of heaven. (That is how it should be today.) If the whole world is going astray and not doing right in GOD's eyesight, each man should consider in his heart and is admonished to turn and follow JESUS by his own convictions. Your salvation is based on your individual walk with GOD, not based on what happens around you!

GOD told Abram, whose name was later changed to Abraham, to leave his father's house and his family and even his country and go to a place where he did not have any idea where he was going. **"Now the LORD had said unto Abram, get thee out of thy country, and from thy kindred, and from** thy father's house, unto a land where I will show thee: And I will make of thee a great nation, and I will bless thee, and make thy name great; and thou shalt be a blessing: And I will bless them that bless thee, and curse him that curseth thee: <u>and in thee shall all families of the earth be blessed</u>." Gen. 12:1–3

Today, it seems, people cannot do half of what GOD instructs them to do when they know exactly what is required of them. There is an urgent need to start following GOD at His word and obeying His word alone at this present time. Not until this is done will perfect peace be found. Abraham followed GOD and God told him, "<u>**And in thy seed shall all the nations of the earth be blessed**</u>;" Why? "<u>**because thou hast obeyed My voice**</u>." Gen. 22:18 The promise of the coming Messiah was given to Abraham that through his bloodline, through his seed, shall the Redeemer of all the earth and fallen man come forth simply because of his faith and obedience to GOD when He spoke.

Abraham, along with his wife Sarah, had a son according to the promise of GOD. When GOD promises a thing, you can surely bank on it! Amen? **"And GOD said, 'Sarah thy wife shall bear thee a son indeed; and thou shalt call his name Isaac: and I will establish My covenant with him for an everlasting covenant and with his seed after him'."** Gen. 17:19

All the nations of the earth were to be blessed through Abraham's son Isaac. **"For in Isaac shall thy seed be called."** Gen. 21:12

It is worth mentioning that maybe if Sarah's heart was right from the beginning, Abraham and herself would not have had to wait as long as they did to have their son Isaac. GOD knew what was truly in her heart had to be manifested and brought to light in order for Him to proceed with His plan of salvation. Sarah could not wait holistically putting her trust in GOD, and sure enough the magnitude of her impatience showed up. As so often is today, Sarah wanted to make things happen for herself. Maybe she was attempting to establish the bloodline herself by giving her handmaid Hagar to her husband. The promise for the redemption of all people was to come through the son of Abraham's wife Sarah, not through Ishmael, the son of the bondwoman Hagar. **"-for in Isaac shall thy seed be called."** Gen. 21:12

Hagar was promised however, that her son Ishmael would become a great nation because he too was the seed of Abraham. **"Arise, lift up the lad, and hold him in thine hand; for I will make him a great nation."** Gen. 21:18 which indeed took place, but again we see that the lineage of the promised Messiah came by way of Isaac. Because of Sarah's impatience and inability to wait on GOD, there is, to this very day, discord in the Middle East against Israel and terrorism in most parts of the world that is directly related to this mistake on her part. For it was mentioned of Ishmael's offspring, **"And he will be a wild man; his hand will be against every man, and every man's hand against him; and he shall dwell in the presence of all his brethren."** Gen. 16:12

One of the tests (trials) that were imposed upon Abraham to see how his reaction would be and thereby reflect to whom he gave his devotion. Whether he gave himself over to heavenly things; that is to the God of all creation or to the cares of this world and to Satan. One of the severest tests that could be imposed upon any man in his right mind, Abraham would have to endure. As was the case, Abraham stepped up to the plate and passed the test with flying colors. GOD said unto Abraham, **"Take now thy son, thine only son Isaac, whom thou lovest, and get into the land of Moriah; and offer him there for a burnt offering upon one of the mountains which I will tell thee of."** Gen. 22:2

Needless to say, Abraham got up and went as instructed. He never questioned GOD or charged GOD foolishly. He had been used to communing with GOD and knew His voice. He knew that the other nations around him were passing their children through the fire to Molech in worship to him and other false gods. He knew GOD, and he knew that the promised Redeemer had to come through his son Isaac because he also knew that GOD does not lie. Another thing that Abraham knew without really knowing how was the fact that GOD could provide and make a way even when it appears to the physical senses that there is no way. Abraham knew that somehow he and his son would return. **"And Isaac spake unto Abraham his father, and said, 'My father': and he said, 'Here am I my son.' And he said, 'Behold the fire and the wood; but where is the lamb for a burnt offering?' And Abraham said, 'My son GOD will provide for Himself a lamb for a burnt offering.'"** Gen. 22:7 and 8

Abraham had bound Isaac to the sacrificial altar and had the glittering knife posed over head with the intent to strike his son. When GOD spoke, **"Abraham, Abraham; And Abraham said, 'Here am I.' And GOD said, 'Lay not thine hand upon the lad, neither do thou anything unto him; for now I know that thou fearest GOD, seeing thou hast not with-held thy son, thine only son from me.'"** Gen. 22:11 and 12

The unconditional promise GOD had made that through Abraham's seed all the families of the earth would be blessed could at this point now go forward.

Isaac grew up and married a very pretty and fair young lady named Rebekah. But all the while, Isaac, as did Abraham, never strayed from following GOD, and he obeyed GOD's voice. So GOD to Isaac reconfirmed the promise. **"For unto thee, and unto thy seed, I will give all these countries, and I will perform the oath which I sware unto Abraham thy father."** Gen. 26:3 **And I will make thy seed as the stars of heaven, and will give unto thy seed all these countries; <u>and in thy seed shall all the nations of the earth be blessed."</u>** (Not only for the Jews but through the Jewish lineage our Savior was to come for all people. And please keep in mind that the term Jew has not surfaced at this point in time.) **Because that Abraham <u>obeyed</u> My voice, and kept My charge, My commandments, My statutes, and My laws."** Gen. 26:3–5

Because the promise was continued through Isaac and because Isaac was not the promised redeemer, Isaac had to have at least one child or the covenant for the redemption of all mankind stops with him. God's word is true, and prophecy cannot be altered. **"The entrance of Thy words giveth light; it giveth understanding unto the simple."** Ps. 119:130

Rebekah bore Isaac a set of twins. With God, there was no need of an ultrasound machine as needed today to know beforehand what the sex of children before birth would be. The LORD gave her spiritual ultrasound and told her she would have twins and what sex they would be. But He, being the mighty GOD that He is, went further than that and even told her the nature of the two sons and also the outcome of their lives in the future. He told her exactly what manner of people both of them would become. Man, with all of his technological wizardry, does not have the availability without any doubt to see or to predict with one hundred percent certainty one second into the future. Doctors today may be able to tell you with some degree of accuracy the sex of the unborn child, but I don't know of any that can tell you what manner of child they would be and over the years exactly how their lives would turn out. GOD on the other hand is able to, and He did. **"And the LORD said unto her, 'Two nations are in thy womb, and two manner of people shall be separated from thy bowels; and the one people shall be stronger than the other people; and the elder shall serve the younger'. And when her days to be delivered were fulfilled, behold, there were twins in her womb."** Gen. 25:23 and 24

As God said she would, Rebekah gave birth to a set of twins: Esau, the elder and Jacob, the younger. This story is well-known. Esau sold his birthright to his younger brother for some soup. (How often are we selling ourselves over to something of this world?) The blessing of the promised Savior would ultimately come through the lineage of Jacob as prophesied, and looking back, there can be no doubt as to the outcome of this particular pregnancy developing exactly as God said it would. The elder shall serve the younger.

Again Jacob, as did his fathers before him, served God with a whole heart. But Jacob was not the catalyst (the Redeemer) to come. Therefore, he too had to have an offspring to fulfill the promise. Jacob had a dream in the form of a ladder that stretched up into heaven from the earth. GOD was at the head of the ladder, and His ministering spirits (angels) were ascending and descending on it. This ladder represented the connection between GOD and man, His Son Christ Jesus. This ladder represented the promised redeemer to come, and again like his fathers before him, the promise was again confirmed to Jacob by GOD. **"And thy seed shall be as the dust of the earth, and you shall spread abroad to the west, and to the east, and to the north, and to the south: and in you and in your seed <u>shall all the families of the earth be blessed</u>."** Gen. 28:14

Jacob had deceived Isaac, his father, by pretending to be his older twin brother Esau in order to receive the firstborn's blessing from Isaac, which he thought he was giving to his older son. If Jacob had not gain the blessings by deception and patiently waited, he some way would have still received them in order to fulfill the prophecy and promise. "The elder will serve the younger." Needless to say, when he found out what Jacob had done, Esau was not at all well pleased. Over an extended period of time, the two brothers had been separated, and now the time had come for them to meet face to face again.

Jacob was afraid to meet Esau his brother because after all, he had only taken by deception, his big brother's birthright and his blessing. But he had forgotten one thing. God had already made Jacob a few promises that he could bank on. There was, in all actuality, no need for him to worry. But this was a test-tube experience for Jacob; experimentation if you will that he had to overcome.

The night before Jacob was to meet his brother Esau, Jacob had separated his family and the people that were with him into two companies led by each of his two wives and sent them across the brook that was near where they were. He was left alone, and that night the LORD wrestled with Jacob.

This particular night, Jacob's name was changed to Israel because he had wrestled with a power higher than himself and prevailed. Because he was to be the father of God's chosen nation of people, who were to lead all nations to the true God. The name intrinsically implies that 'GOD **IS** REAL!' (ISRAEL) But scriptures reveal exactly what the name means, "And he said, 'Thy name shall be called no more Jacob, but Israel: for as a prince hast thou power with God and with men, and hast prevailed.'" Gen. 32:28

A new nation is born. A new nation that had not previously existed is now called Israel of which the promised Redeemer would come through. This new nation was to be a peculiar people to represent GOD in the earth. It would be different from all of the surrounding nations. It was to be a kingdom of priest and to be a lighthouse for other countries of the earth. It was to demonstrate GOD's will and love as well as be the instrumental nation to promulgate His plan of salvation for all men. In other words, Israel was to be God's guiding light to be used to fulfill all of His purposes of love.

The nation of Israel was to reveal GOD's character to the rest of the world. They were to reflect the will of GOD so that the whole world might be one big happy family of believers in the only true GOD. If this representation had been done the way God had intended, then the entire planet Earth would have been in harmony with the rest of the universe in worship and allegiance to Almighty GOD. Can you imagine one big universal Sabbath? All created beings coming together in harmony to worship the creator as one big happy family. Get used to the thought because this is exactly how it is going to be after Christ's return. It will be how He intended it to be at the first. **"And it shall come to pass, that from one new moon to another, and from one Sabbath to another, shall all flesh come to worship before me, saith the LORD."** Isa. 66:23 Again, **"One Lord, one faith, and one baptism."** Eph. 4:5

The nations surrounding Israel had other gods they worshipped, and they believed that they had then, as some religions think today, the true God and the right religion. The GOD of Israel did not exclude anyone from coming to Him in the truth. After all that was one of Israel's primary directives. They were to evangelize the entire world letting them know who the true God was. It was as true back then as it is today; Israel could only reflect the true God they could not on the other hand force God upon anyone. It was up to the surrounding nations to decide for themselves whether or not they would follow God's way and to become a part of the family of believers.

If a stranger was within the gates of Israel and he followed the practices of the nation, then he was entitled to the same benefits as a home-born Israelite. There should not have been any difference between the stranger and the Israelite citizen, spiritual or otherwise. This unprejudiced philosophy was to apply to any one individual, nation, people, or language that came into Israel's gatherings. **"And if a stranger sojourns with you in your land, you shall not vex him. [But] the stranger that dwells with you shall be unto you as one born among you, and you shall love him as yourself; for you were strangers in the land of Egypt: I [am] the LORD your God."** Lev. 19:33 and 34 **"One law and one manner shall be for you, and for the stranger that sojourns with you."** Num. 15:16 And it is as true today as it was then, that if *all* men believed in the promised Redeemer given to the lineage of Abraham and follow the practices outlined in His sacred word, everyone on this test-tube planet would have a right to the tree of life. **"Blessed are they who do His commandments that they may have right to the tree of life, and enter in through the gates into the city."** Rev. 22:14 This blessing is open to everyone. Not one is excluded if they adhere to Christ following His commandments as outlined in the preceding text.

Again, the promise was not for the children of Israel alone as some of them may be inclined to believe. No one is excluded. You do not have to be of a particular sect or creed. It does not matter what race you are or what nationality you belong to; you are as good to go if you believe in the promised Redeemer and keep His commandments. It is the greatness and the zeal of the Lord of hosts who is able to do this. He made a way for all men, and all that has to be done is to accept it and follow the plan. Follow the redemptive blueprint right into heaven! Amen.

Jacob, who is now Israel, had twelve sons: Reuben, his firstborn; then Simeon, Levi, Judah, Dan, Naphtali, Gad, Asher, Issachar, Zebulon, Joseph, and Benjamin. These constituted the twelve tribes of Israel. One of these twelve, according to the promise made by God, had to be the progenitor or avenue by which the promised Redeemer, the Lamb slain from the foundation of the world comes through and manifests Himself.

God wanted to accomplish this particular promise through the firstborn but as was often the case, God almost always used a second or a younger son to manifest His promises. As with the twelve sons of Jacob, Reuben, the firstborn, did not follow the plan and had deviated from the will of GOD; an alternative had to be selected. You know the story in the book of Genesis where Reuben, the firstborn, solicited one of Jacob's concubines (Belhah) to have sex with her and thereby relinquishing his right to the birthright. Going upon his father's skirts or looking upon his father's nakedness was not pleasing to God. **"The nakedness of thy father, or the nakedness of thy mother, shalt thou not uncover: she is thy mother; thou shalt not uncover her nakedness. The nakedness of thy father's wife shalt thou not uncover: It is thy father's nakedness."** Lev. 18:7 and 8

It stands to reason that Simeon was the second born and would be next in line and chosen of God to fulfill His promises made to Abraham, Isaac, and Jacob for the entire world, **"And I will bless them that bless thee, and curse him that curseth thee: and in thee shall all families of the earth be blessed."** Gen. 12:3

However, the next two in line, Simeon and Levi, betrayed their father Jacob's trust by dealing contrary to his will with Hamor and his son Shechem by taking up the sword against them. Shechem had defiled Dinah, their sister, by having a sexual encounter with her when they were not married. Shechem loved Dinah though and had set up an agreement for them to marry. Simeon and Levi had abused their father Jacob's promise of peace. When the men of Shechem had agreed to follow the custom of circumcision and live peaceably with Israel exchanging wives one with another, Jacob's second and third sons dealt treacherously with them by attacking them as the men of Shechem were weak after being circumcised. **"And it came to pass on the third day, when they were sore, that two of the sons of Jacob, Simeon and Levi, Dinah's brothers, took each man his sword, and came upon the city boldly, and slew all the males."** Gen. 34:25 **(It is interesting to note that it was unsanctioned sexual activities that caused Jacob to be at odds with his first three sons. How many of us is the Heavenly Father at odds with because of lustful sexual activities?)**

Because of this treacherous betrayal, Jacob's next two sons could not be used to fulfill the promises of Almighty God. It was by divine order, providence, and keeping things in perfect sequential order that the line used for the entrance of the Messiah into the world would not come through Joseph as many believe but would come through the next in line, the fourth son of Jacob, which was the mighty tribe of Judah! **"And one of the elders saith unto me, 'Weep not, behold, the Lion of the tribe of JUDAH, the Root of David, hath prevailed to open the book, and to loose the seven seals thereof'"** .Rev. 5:5 The promised Redeemer is called The Lion of the tribe of Judah. Not the Lion of the tribe of Joseph.

It was through this line of Judah Jacob's fourth son whose name means "praise be to God" that Jesus Christ the Savior of the world would and did come. However, another item of note is though Judah was next in line for the promise, the first four sons of Jacob were by Leah and not by Rachel whom he loved most. **"And Jacob loved Rachel; and said, 'I will serve thee seven years for Rachel thy younger daughter.'"** Gen. 29:18

It is so amazing how by God's grace, He still used Jacob's firstborn by the woman whom he loved most. Joseph had done nothing to vanquish his father nor had he done anything against God. As a matter of fact, because Joseph was such an obedient child, his father set him more favorable than his brothers and presented him with a physical representation of this honor by giving him a special coat. **"Now Israel loved Joseph more than all his children, because he was the son of his old age: and he made him a coat of many colours."** Gen. 37:3

Joseph was the instrument by which God used to accomplish a major prophecy and promise He had made to Abraham many years before. **"And He said unto Abram, 'Know of a surety that thy seed shall be a stranger in a land that is not theirs, and shall serve them; and they shall afflict them four hundred years. And also that nation, whom they shall serve, will I judge: and afterward shall they come out with great substance'."** Gen. 15:13 and 14

Joseph's name implies "God shall add to his people." It was to Egyptian slave traders which Joseph was sold into slavery that the nation of Israel grew and became in very deed a great nation unto God. **"And He said, 'I am God, the God of thy father: fear not to go down into Egypt; for I will there make of thee a great nation.'"** Gen. 46:3

By the providence of God, Joseph was used to fulfill the prophecy God had given to Abraham that for four hundred years, his seed or offspring should serve a people in a strange land. Joseph was not Jacob's firstborn per se, but he was the firstborn of Rachel, the wife whom Jacob loved most. That prophecy began to be fulfilled when Joseph was sold into slavery by his brethren and carried down into Egypt. What they thought to be harmful to Joseph really was eventually for their good. It was through this act of selfishness and treachery that the providential word of God was to be fulfilled. Because of what Jacob's brothers did unto him, eventually, the entire tribe of Israel ended up in Egypt, and it was there after a period of time that they became slaves to the house of Pharaoh and remained there for a little over four hundred years.

After a king rose up who knew not Joseph and saw the people of Israel growing beyond measure, he caused the children of Israel to go into hard bondage and serve the Egyptians with vigorous labor. Another observation is that Jacob's sons sold Joseph into slavery, and he was in Egypt for about twenty years before Jacob was brought to him. Jacob's sons make up the tribes that constitute the nation of Israel. They served in Egypt for about twenty years per year that Jacob was there. Twenty times twenty equals four hundred (20 x 20 = 400).

It was then after the prescribed time of servitude and the nation grew that the Lord raised up Moses of the seed of Levi, whom GOD used to deliver His chosen ones out of Egypt. Again notice that Moses was not the firstborn of Amram and Jochebed, his parents, for Moses had an older brother named Aaron. Moses, the younger brother, was used for the purposes of revealing God's might and to receive His glory. GOD, in His mighty power, parted the Red Sea and led His children safely through the mist of the waters. No harm came upon them but to those who opposed His truth met their final fate that day. The Egyptian army was overwhelmed and destroyed by the same Red Sea used for the safe passage of God's people. Prior to that fateful day, Egypt ruled the then-known world, but that day when the Egyptian host met the heavenly host at the Red Sea, the Great GOD of Heaven dealt a crushing blow to the Egyptian army. **"And the sea returned to his strength when the morning appeared; and the Egyptians fled against it; and the LORD overthrew the Egyptians in the midst of the sea. And the waters returned, and covered the chariots, and the horsemen, [and] all the host of Pharaoh that came into the sea after them; there remained not so much as one of them."** Ex. 14:27 and 28

That day could have possibly been the last of the Egyptians rising up to be a world-ruling nation. Moses was instructed, once reaching the other side of the sea, to lead the body of believers to Mount Sinai to receive GOD's Ten Commandments written with the finger of God Himself (the Law of the Covenant). Moses had been up in the mountain for approximately forty days, and some of the hardheaded, hard-hearted children had already apostatized. They had only, a few weeks ago, seen GOD operate with a mighty hand at the Red Sea and had forgotten that quickly exactly what He had done for them. Many people today do the same thing. They forget how GOD has delivered them in times past and backslide into apostasy, sometimes very quickly and oftentimes never to return.

Not long after the splitting of the Red Sea along with the exodus of God's people from Egypt, a large number of them began turning aside from the leading of God and began congregating in unrighteousness and making an idol god in the form of a golden calf. This was according to them, their god that brought them up out of the land of Egypt. **"They have turned aside quickly out of the way which I commanded them: they have made them a molten calf, and have worshipped it, and have sacrificed thereunto, and said, 'These be thy gods, O Israel, which have brought thee out of the land of Egypt.'"** Ex. 32:8 How absurd?

How often do we set up golden calves in our lives to go before us? In the form of relationships, we put ahead of GOD. Not to mention jobs, careers, houses, fine cars, money, and even food just to name a few of the idols that can be set up in the heart! Unconsciously, these selfish desires and worldly possessions get more homage from would-be Christians (not to mention unbelievers) than do Almighty GOD Himself, especially the economic or financial portions of their lives. Think about it for a moment. On any given day, what occupies or consumes most of your thoughts? Just like some of the backsliding Israelites, some of us would fail the test and like them be destroyed. There is no difference. It is very important to be conscientiously aware of testing and trials and to not be overtaking by them. Salvation is very much dependent on and directly proportional to overcoming trials and temptations.

God, with his love for man, wanted to live with him, so He instructed Moses to build Him a sanctuary. **"And let them make Me a Sanctuary; that I may dwell among them."** Ex. 25:8

The sanctuary, along with Israel's worship services and their lifestyle, was to indicate that they were GOD's chosen people and they were to be a peculiar people in the eyes of the nations surrounding them. In other words, the children of Israel's Godly lifestyles should have been a witness to all around them, even if they never said a word to their neighbors. Christians today should reflect a similar differential character in their deportments than that of the world. The children of Israel were to reflect GOD's true character and to lead all people to the throne of the one true GOD. It was also GOD's purpose that all nations of the world would worship Him as did Israel, and they were to lead the way. **"Now therefore, if you will obey My voice indeed, and keep My covenant, then ye shall be a peculiar treasure unto Me above all people: for all the earth is Mine. And ye shall be unto Me a kingdom of priest, and a Holy nation."** Ex. 19:5 and 6

This peculiarity of GOD's people did not become extinguished at the death and resurrection of Jesus either. Christians today should have an appearance and an outward reflection of a different disposition than the rest of the world. As did Christ, His disciples, the early church, the true Christians during the Dark Ages and as all who profess the name of Christ should be in this day and time. **"If you were of the world, the world would love his own; but because you are not of the world, but I have chosen you out of the world, therefore the world hates you."** Jn. 15:19

A child of GOD should appear in a nice respectable and wholesome way, different than the rest of the world in their daily business transactions and deportments. There should be a noticeable difference in every aspect of life. Christians today should reflect some character of peculiarity or differences from the rest of the world as God has placed on his first church, the children of Israel to be a peculiar treasure, a kingdom of priests, and a holy nation of people in the earth. Also in this dispensation, Christians should uphold a godly deportment representing the character of the true GOD of heaven. **"But ye are a chosen generation, a royal priesthood, a holy nation, a peculiar people; that ye should show forth the praises of Him who hath called you out of darkness into His marvelous light."** 1 Pet. 2:9

The sanctuary that Moses was instructed to build was a sight to behold in the midst of the congregation of the people. It was funded by a freewill offering and was to be constructed of definite proportions. The eastern and western sides were of equal width. The northern and southern sides were of equal length. The later sides being longer than the former, therefore, the structure was of rectangular dimensions.

Because the children of Israel were a mobile people at the time the sanctuary was to be constructed, it was to be constructed in a tabernacle form, sort of like a big tent. This was done so that it could be readily deconstructed and moved when need be. All of the furniture and services of the sanctuary were construed of an elaborate set of types and symbols representing the Messiah to come and of the Christian experience.

The sanctuary consisted of three compartments surrounded by a fence of curtains: the outer court, the Holy Place, and the Most Holy Place where GOD's actual presence resides. The only entrance into the sanctuary was through the eastern side of which upon entering, places you into the outer court and as you traverse westward in a straight line, you would pass beyond the first veil leading you into the inner court or Holy Place, continuing on straight ahead past the second veil and eventually ending up in the Most Holy Place in the presence of Almighty GOD.

From an earthly perspective and God being a God of consistency, the same GOD who established the heavens and the earth, gave the appearance of the sun to rise, on a daily basis, begin its journey from the east, traverse through the sky in a westward straight-line fashion and terminate or set in the west ending its daily representation of the Christian walk. The resemblance of this pattern is not accidental. Christ's return will be much in the same manner further establishing the consistency of GOD who never changes. **"For as the lightning cometh out of the east, and shineth even unto the west; so shall also the coming of the Son of man be."** Matt. 24:27

We too, in our Christian experience, should be making a westward life's journey in Christ Jesus. Amen. Christ said for us to come unto Him, (that is beginning in the east at the outer court) but after we come, that is not enough. He said to learn of Him (that is, traversing through the Holy Place to the Most Holy Place). Taking on more and more of the character of Christ and representing Him in thoughts and actions until you are sealed to His second coming is your westward journey. Evolving by sanctification into that peculiar people and royal priesthood that Christ would have true Christians to be in the earth. Like the sun turning neither to the left nor to the right but straight into the Kingdom of God! From east to west!

Again, the sanctuary and everything pertaining to it points to Christ and His work. Upon entering at the eastern gate, you would be standing in the outer court; the first thing you would see is the altar of burnt offering (the brazen altar). This is where the typical sacrificial offerings are offered up unto GOD. Some of the blood was taken from the innocent victim (sacrificial animal) that was being slain and placed in a bowl to be brought within the sanctuary by the ministering priest or some of the flesh would be eaten by the priest. In any event, the sin was brought into the sanctuary. The innocent victim was being sacrificed in place of the one who had committed the sinful acts. It represented the antitypical true sacrifice Jesus Christ the Lamb of GOD slain from the foundation of the world would make for the repentant sinner. When a person comes to Christ, it is this true sacrifice that enables the sinner to come to GOD and to be purged of sin. **"How much more shall the blood of CHRIST, who through the eternal SPIRIT <u>offered</u> Himself without spot to GOD, purged your conscience from dead works to serve the living GOD?"** Heb. 9:14

After the brazen altar as you walk westward, you would encounter the laver and its foot. This is an artifice used by priests to wash and cleanse their hands and feet before entering the Holy Place. **"Not by works of righteousness, which we have done, but according to His mercy He saved us, by the <u>washing</u> of regeneration, and renewing of the Holy Ghost. Which He shed on us abundantly through Jesus Christ our Saviour."** Tit. 3:5 and 6

It is Christ who is the Laver of life that cleanses us from all unrighteousness and set us on straight paths. **"Create in me a clean heart, O God; and renew a right spirit within me."** Ps. 51:10

Passing the laver, you would proceed and come before the veil that leads into the second compartment—the inner court or the Holy Place. If you looked to the right on the northern side of the sanctuary, you would see a table with shewbread (showbread) on it. This bread signifies the bread of the presence. This bread representing ever-present Jesus Christ, the true bread of life, was to be changed every day and to be eaten only by the serving priests. **"And Jesus said unto them, 'I am the <u>bread of life</u>: he that cometh to Me shall never hunger; and he that believeth on Me shall never thirst.'"** Jn. 6:35

Looking to the left while facing west, you would see the seven-branched golden candlestick on the southern side of the Holy Place. According to scriptures, this too represents the savior. **"These things saith He that holdeth the seven stars in His right hand, Who walketh in the midst of the seven golden candlesticks."** Rev. 2:1 **"The seven stars are the angels of the seven churches: and the seven candlesticks which thou sawest are the seven churches."** Rev. 1:20 Christ is indeed the head of the church and walketh in the midst of it. **"For the husband is the head of the wife, even as Christ is the head of the church: and He is the Saviour of the body."** Eph. 5:23 (Please bear in mind that the seven churches represented by the seven golden candle sticks are not seven different denominations but one church body of seven different localities.)However, in the typical services, the seven-bowled lamp stand was also used for lighting purposes within the sanctuary, but Christ too is our light and the light of the world. **"Then spoke Jesus again unto them, saying, 'I am the light of the world: he that follows Me shall not walk in darkness, but shall have the light of life.'"** Jn. 8:12

Looking straight ahead in the westward direction right before the veil is the altar of incense which can be seen and the rising smoke from the alter represents the prayers of the saints that ascend up to Christ Jesus who mediates in our behalf. I am sure glad of that. How about you? **"For there is one God, and one mediator between GOD and men, the man CHRIST JESUS."** 1 Tim. 2:5 **"And the smoke of the incense, which came with the prayers of the saints, ascended up before GOD out of the angel's hand."** Rev. 8:4

As you continue your journey through the earthly sanctuary, you would behold a thick veil that is directly behind the altar of incense. The smoke of the incense would scale up the veil and over the top going into the Most Holy Place again representing the prayers of the saints and to be a sweet savor unto our GOD. The veil stretches across the entire width of the sanctuary from north to south separating the inner court (the Holy Place) from the Holy of Holies (the Most Holy Place). On a daily basis, the common priests could not see behind this veil because from end to end, there was no gap to view behind it. And as usual with much consistency, you would find a representation of the SON of GOD concerning this veil. **"Which hope we have as an anchor of the soul, both sure and steadfast, and which entered into that within the <u>veil</u>; Whither the forerunner is for us entered, even JESUS, made an high priest for ever after the order of Melchisedec."** Heb. 6:19 and 20

The common priests administered the services of the sanctuary daily. Throughout the year, day by day, they burned sacrifices on the brazen altar for themselves and for the people in the outer court. The common priests also served within the Holy Place on a daily basis. They kept the shewbread fresh and in order. The lamps were trimmed, and fresh oil was continuously supplied. (The oil represents the HOLY SPIRIT.) And prayers were offered up by way of the altar of incense before the veil day and night for all the children of Israel. This takes care of the first two sections of the sanctuary (the outer court and the inner court).

The last compartment of the sanctuary is the Holy of Holies or the Most Holy Place. Once behind the veil, you would behold the Ark of the Covenant of which the grace of GOD extends all the way back to the Garden of Eden, right up to the cross, and on down to the close of probation to the second coming of Jesus. Again, this ark contained the Law of the Covenant, the Ten Commandments, not the law of Moses. At the close of probation, this grace of GOD ceases to be extended to man any further. **"He that is unjust, let him be unjust still; and he that is filthy, let him be filthy still:**

And he that is righteous, let him be righteous still; And he that is holy, let him be holy still." Rev. 22:11

That's right, friend, there is a day rapidly approaching when this earth will rock and reel like a drunkard and the elements are going to melt with fervent heat. Preference for GOD's grace as opposed to His wrath which will be poured out without mixture should be of high priority, especially to those who claim the title of Christian. **"The same shall drink of the wine of the wrath of God, which is poured out without mixture into the cup of His indignation; and he shall be tormented with fire and brimstone in the presence of the holy angels, and in the presence of the Lamb:"** Rev. 14:10

Once a year on the Day of Atonement, (at-one-ment with GOD) the high priest that was selected for that year went behind the veil. He wore a breastplate with twelve different precious stones set in it. Each stone represented a specific tribe of Israel. The high priest would wear this breastplate over their ephod on the Day of Atonement before he went behind the veil and consequently in the very presence of the Almighty's Shechinah Glory.

The Day of Atonement was a very anticipatory day and a very solemn one. A specific alarm (the blowing of trumpets) was sounded ten days prior to the Day of Atonement. This day was called the "blowing of the trumpets" and was sort of an alarm clock or a reminder if you will. This was done so that the entire congregation would not be caught off guard nor have an excuse to say they did not know the Day of Atonement was coming. They had ten days to sanctify and prepare themselves for the day of their cleansing. **"In the seventh month, in the first day of the month, shall ye have a Sabbath, a memorial of blowing of trumpets, a Holy Convocation."** Lev. 23:24 **"Also, on the tenth day of this seventh month there should be a Day of Atonement: it shall be an Holy Convocation unto you; and ye shall afflict your souls, and offer an offering made by fire unto the LORD."** Lev. 23:27

Remember, like evaporated water, sin once committed does not simply disappear. Someone has to account for the sinful act committed. Someone has to pay for that committed sin (namely, the sinner). All during the year, day by day, sin had been transferred from the sinner to the innocent victim. The sacrificial animal's blood would be carried into the Holy Place and transferred into the sanctuary by the priest. Thus, the sins of the people (the sinners) were transferred from the sin-filled world inside to the sanctuary where they remained until the Day of Atonement. Up until the Day of Atonement, the sins of the people had been transferred from the sinner to the sanctuary but had not been eradicated. Again, ten days before on the first day of the seventh month, an alarm was to be sounded. The people were to prepare and sanctify their hearts for the upcoming day of cleansing. It was only on the Day of Atonement the high priest was allowed to go behind the veil to see whether or not their sacrifices and services (the way they walked before the LORD) were accepted.

Before entering the sanctuary, two goats were selected. Lots had been drawn to determine which would be the scapegoat and which would be the LORD's goat. The LORD's goat would be offered as a sacrifice, and some of the blood would be taken into the sanctuary to be administered there for sanctification purposes. Without going into full detail (this is not the scope of this book), if GOD was pleased with everything, it would be acknowledged by the high priest, and the sin-stained blood that had been placed within the sanctuary all year would be miraculously cleansed from the sanctuary. In other words, the sins are now being dealt with. However, at this point, the sins still are not eradicated. They still exist at this point. The questions should come to mind, "Where are all of these committed but confessed and forgiven sins?" "Where did they go?" The forgiven sins of all the people for that year had been removed from the sanctuary and placed upon the high priest. The high priest then moves out from the presence of Almighty God in a backward motion out of the Most Holy Place; he then turns around and traverses through the Holy Place and outer court. He is now outside of the sanctuary where the live scapegoat is. The high priest places his hands over the head of the only goat that remains. With his hands placed over the head of the live goat (scapegoat) all of the sins of the forgiven sinners are transferred from the high priest upon the head of the scapegoat. The scapegoat, now burdened with all of the forgiven sins of the people, would be led into the wilderness by a fit man (strong man) never to return again into the camp. He is left out there to die an un-sanctimonious and lonely death. At this point, God's grace has rain down like a mighty stream. The sins of the forgiven are indeed eradicated and never to be mentioned again. Hallelujah! A just God, a forgiving God, a merciful God has done this! **"And Aaron shall lay both his hands upon the head of the live goat, and confess over him all the iniquities of the children of Israel, and all their transgressions in all their sins, putting them upon the head of the goat, and shall send him away by the hand of a fit man into the wilderness: And the goat shall bear upon him all their iniquities unto a land not inhabited: and he shall let go the goat in the wilderness."** Lev. 16:21 and 22

"He will turn again, He will have compassion upon us; He will subdue our iniquities; and thou wilt cast all their sins into the depths of the sea." Mic. 7:19

This again points to the true heavenly sanctuary where Christ, our High Priest, pleads for a lost world day and night. He takes the sins of the repentant sinner, and at the end of the world, all of the forgiven sins of all those who will be saved are upon Him. Those whose sins will be taken from the sanctuary by our High Priest, CHRIST, and placed upon HIM will at the end place them upon the head of the devil, the antitypical or true scapegoat, and it is he that will ultimately burn for those sins. Lead away to a lake of fire burning with brimstone by a Mighty God never to return again, he is forever destroyed.

At the end of the world, Jesus will not have the sins of the unrepentant, the wicked, and those who have not confessed their sins. They will, with much regret of the true High Priest by default of their own choosing, burn for their own iniquities. Everyone from every persuasion of all religious sects and organizations who followed not God at His Word along with those who do not believe in God fall into this category, simply for the fact that there has to be a blood atonement for every sin. "The wages of sin is death." And though innocent, the blood from any animal just simply cannot atone. Therefore an innocent victim with the credentials and power to atone must make atonement for the sinner and this happens to be Jesus Christ the Son of God. **"For God so loved the world that He gave His only begotten Son, that whosoever believeth in Him shall not perish but have everlasting life."** John 3:16 **"And the devil that deceived them was cast into the lake of fire and brimstone; And death and hell were cast into the lake of fire. This is the second death. And whosoever was not found written in the book of life was cast into the lake of fire."** Rev. 20:10, 14 and 15

The last compartment of the sanctuary has more to be examined. Above the ark in the Most Holy Place was a lid or a covering that is called the Mercy Seat. On top of the Mercy Seat were two cherubim that faced one another with their wings outstretched over the ark and touching each other over the midst of the ark. They reverently look down toward the Mercy Seat where directly underneath reside the contents of the ark. God's presence at times dwelt between the two cherubim. Underneath the Mercy Seat and inside of the ark were three items: (1) the Law of the Covenant (The Ten Commandments); (2) a small pot of manna that GOD gave the children of Israel from the ovens of Heaven. **"Our fathers did eat manna in the desert; as it is written, He gave them bread from Heaven to eat. Then Jesus said unto them, 'Verily, verily, I say unto you, Moses gave you not that bread from Heaven; but My Father giveth you the true bread from Heaven.'"** Jn. 6:31 and 32 (3) Aaron's rod that budded with almond blossoms and almonds to establish the tribe of Levi as the priest of the sanctuary forever before the Lord. The same pointed toward JESUS, the true high priest. **"And** being made perfect, He became the author of eternal salvation unto all them that obey Him; called of GOD an <u>High Priest</u> after the order of Melchisedec." Heb. 5:9 and 10

Please remember that the first item placed into the ark was GOD's Ten Commandments. As a matter of note, the ark was originally designed to hold only the Ten Commandments. It was not until other events took place that the other two items were instructed to be placed inside the ark with God's Commandments as reminders for future generations. Again, everything inside of the ark represented CHRIST. The Ten Commandments written with the finger of GOD on two tables of stone spelled out His character to a faltering world. **"And the <u>WORD</u> was made flesh, and dwelt amongst us, [and we beheld His glory, the glory as of the only begotten of the Father,] full of grace and truth."** Jn. 1:14

There is a need for the world of Christians to recognize that not seven, eight, or even nine but all TEN of God's law must be obeyed and kept. They cannot be kept in human power, but they can be kept in the power of Christ! It is unacceptable to keep only the ones that you are comfortable with, but it is necessary to abide by all Ten. **"For whosoever shall keep the whole law, and yet offend in one point, he is guilty of all. For He that said, 'Do not commit adultery,' said also, 'Do not kill.' Now if thou commit no adultery, yet if thou kill, thou art become a transgressor of the law."** James 2:10 and 11

This is not referring to the law of ordination nor the ceremonial laws (Moses's law). This law was nailed to the cross. And this was the only law that was nailed to the cross. **"Blotting out the handwriting of ordinances that was against us, which was contrary to us, and took it out of the way nailing it to His cross."** Col. 2:14

A point of clarity needs to be made here, even the laws of ordinances and ceremonies were not holistically done away with it is simply that type have met anti-type and there was no longer any need for the commencement of the sacrificial services or ceremonies. The true had come, and all representation of the true had been fulfilled. However, GOD's character, reflected by the WORD of GOD, which is CHRIST JESUS our LORD as seen in the Ten Commandments, has not been done away with. Contrary to popular belief, which many believe the Ten Commandments were nailed to the cross or done away with as were the ceremonial laws. This is an arch deception and fallacy instigated by the arch deceiver himself. For Jesus Himself said, **"Think not that I am come to destroy the law, or the prophets: I am not come to destroy but to fulfill. For verily I say unto you, 'til heaven and earth pass, one jot or one tittle shall in no wise pass from the law, 'til all be fulfilled."** Matt. 5:17 and 18 And anyone teaching contrary to this needs to be on the safeguard because JESUS goes on to say, **"Whosoever therefore should break one of these least commandments, and shall teach men so, he shall be called the <u>least</u> in the Kingdom of Heaven: but whosoever do and teach them, the same shall be called <u>great</u> in the Kingdom of heaven."** Matt. 5:19 Let us follow GOD at His WORD! Amen.

The Mercy Seat is also where GOD administers His mercy and grace. Thus, the name Mercy Seat is justifiably specified. Notice it is not called the Judgment Seat. God does have a Judgment seat and it will be utilized in the judgment but the seat that is directly over His covenant with man is rightly called the "Mercy Seat." **"And will be gracious to whom I will be gracious, and mercy on whom I will show mercy."** Ex. 33:19 **"And the Lord passed by before him, and proclaimed, 'The LORD, The LORD GOD, merciful and gracious, longsuffering, and abundant in goodness and truth."** Ex. 34:6 Where GOD reside, my friend, there is an abundance of mercy, grace, and truth. And unlike man-made courts here on earth where very little if any pardon exists, where He sits in judgment, there is overflowing mercy and pardon. Praise God for that! And guess what, God does not clench to His blessings with a tight fist like we do down here. Quite on the contrary, His hands are opened wide and His promises are there for the taking if we only believe. **"It is of the LORD's mercies that we are not consumed, because**

His compassion's fail not. They are new every morning: great is Thy faithfulness." Lam. 3:22 and 23

The promise of the coming Redeemer had been further established and exemplified within the sanctuary service. GOD demonstrated to the sons of men exactly why there was a need of blood atonement for sin. **"For the wages of sin is death."** Rom. 6:23 as shown by the slaying of the innocent victim (the lamb). He also showed them how the services were to be carried out and what they truly represented. Almighty God dwelt with the children of men, and He simply did not have to. Beyond giving Himself on the cross, dwelling with the sons of men was a great demonstration of His love for His created beings. Think about it, a holy and almighty God wanting to live among hardheaded and hard-hearted sinners like you and me. People wanting to do things their own way and live by their own standards. It had to be LOVE. It must be LOVE. It's got to be LOVE. I am convinced that it was L-O-V-E why He did this. **"He that loveth not knoweth not GOD; for <u>GOD IS LOVE</u>."** 1 Jn. 4:8

Remember Israel's primary commission as a nation was to proclaim GOD's character to the rest of the world. They did with great fervor for a while but again when human factors i.e., pride of life, cares of this world, selfishness, greed, etc., takes root there are going to be some mess-ups and setbacks. They begin to leave off from following the true GOD of Heaven and to follow men along with their practices. They wanted to do things their own way and still reap the blessings of GOD. *A program like that simply does not work!* The children of Israel instead of being this peculiar people, this peculiar treasure that Almighty GOD had intended for them to be, they begin to look to the left and to the right and wanted to appear like the nations around them. They had long begun to take on some of the characters of these heathen nations and following their practices.

They wanted Samuel to make them a king so they could be like not some of the nations but "like all the nations" around them the Bible proclaims (see 1 Sam. 8:5). As for modern-day Christians, we too should not look to be like the rest of the world in our deportments. **"You shall observe to do therefore as the Lord your God hath commanded you: you shall not turn aside to the right hand or to the left."** Deut. 5:32

They begin to diverge from holy precepts, not only in their spiritual but their governmental practices as well. **"Then all the elders of Israel gathered themselves together, and came to Samuel unto Ramah, and said unto him, 'Behold, thou art old, and thy sons walk not in thy ways: now make us a king to judge us like all the nations.' And the LORD said unto Samuel, 'Harken unto the voice of the people in all that they say unto thee: for they have not rejected thee, but they have rejected ME, that I should not reign over them."** 1 Sam. 8:5 and 7

Here, the GOD of the universe had done so many great things in the sight of the nation of Israel and their forefathers, but they rejected Him and wanted to follow the pattern of men and their own inclinations. This is significant to note because the same self-satisfying will will surface also in your own Christian experiences as well. That is, "By way of selfish desires the King of Heaven is rejected in order to appear like the rest of the world."

The children of Israel over time continued this pattern of attempting to be like the rest of the world (within their test-tube experience) until they as a nation had become spiritually darkened. There were kings that arose to serve the living GOD, but there were more that arose who would not. Finally, the promised Redeemer for mankind, the true King of not only Israel but of the entire universe, did come as foretold and promised to Abraham, Isaac, and Jacob (Israel). The true catalyst that could draw all men back to the living GOD was now come into the world, that is, the test tube of man's experience to see how he would react to it.

THE REDEEMER

he night of CHRIST's birth (the night when the catalyst of righteousness was infused into the test tube), the world laid in thick darkness, while the true light of the world lay quietly in a little manger within a little town called Bethlehem. There could not have been a more fitting place for the Savior of a sin sick world to be born. In one of the smallest nations of the world, in one of the smallest states in the nation, in one of the smallest towns in the state, and within a small compartment in a small stable, He came forth lying in a manger. **"But thou, Bethlehem Ephratah, though thou be little among the thousands of Judah, yet out of thee shall He come forth unto Me that is to be ruler in Israel; Whose going forth have been from old, from everlasting."**Mic. 5:2

The antitypical true Lamb of GOD was born in a stable! An animal barn! As domesticated farm animals (like lambs) are born in stables so was it to be for the true Lamb Himself. How amazing God is! He could have provided any luxurious hospital, hotel, or palace for the birth of His Son because the whole world is His. (Remember after leaving Egypt while He traveled with them and even after they were established in Jerusalem for a while, Jehovah God resided in a tent and did not complain.) Could there have been any other more fitting place for the Lamb of God to be born? The sacrificial Lamb of God was indeed born in an animal's abode (Away in a manger, no crib for His bed, the little LORD JESUS lay down His sweet head!)! **"And this shall be a sign unto you; you shall find the Babe wrapped in swaddling clothes, lying in a manger."** Lk 2:12

The Sacrificial Lamb who was to shed His blood for a sin sick world had in-very-deed made His way down to this dark planet through the lineage of Abraham into this test-tube arena. **"For unto us a Child is born, unto us a Son is given: and the government shall be upon His shoulder: and His name shall be called Wonderful, Counselor, The Mighty GOD, The Everlasting Father, The Prince of Peace. Of the increase of His government and peace there shall be no end, upon the throne of David, and upon his kingdom, to order it, and to establish it with judgment and with justice from henceforth even forever. The <u>zeal</u> of The LORD of hosts will perform this."** Isa. 9:6 and 7

The promise GOD had given Abraham some two thousand years prior was now within the test tube as a catalyst for good and to retard wickedness. He came exactly as prophesied right on time.

According to scripture, it is very interesting to note that absolutely no one from the chosen nation of Israel was aware of the timely birth and first advent of the newly-incoming Messiah. No, not one! From the rich to the poor, from the highly exalted to the lowly, not one was looking for Him as prophecy foretold. There were, however, a few <u>wise</u> men coming from the east that had studied the scriptures and was aware of the star and the time of prophecy that led to the advent of the Savior. **"I shall see Him, but not now: I shall behold Him, but not nigh: there shall come a Star out of Jacob, and a Scepter shall rise out of Israel."** Num. 24:17

There were a few Jewish shepherds keeping watch over their flocks by night. Angels appeared unto them and *told* them where they could find the Child King. These few people are all that were present on earth to honor the birth of our Lord. Something is gravely wrong with that picture. Have you ever wondered why only a handful of folk showed up at the Messiah's coronation and His first advent into this world? A few shepherds and few folk who were not even associated with the then-known church! When there should have been more honorable recognition at least from the church, this was the only human representation for the entire world, let alone the church! Come on! There should have been more fanfare, some kind of fireworks or a ticker-tape parade or something! There was absolutely nothing! There were neither ambassadors of foreign dignitaries, honorary guests, (except for the wise men), nor leaders of the church. This is something to think about. It can be understood to some extent, if the world did not herald in the Savior's birth but for the church (Israel) to lay asleep after they were given all the prophecies of His coming! Would it have been any different with the Christian Church today? Is today's Christian Church asleep for the second advent of the soon-coming Savior? It is high time to wake up! **"And that, knowing the time, that now it is high time to awake out of sleep: for now is our salvation nearer than when we believed. The night is far spent, the day is at hand: let us therefore cast off the works of darkness, and let us put on the armor of light."** Rom. 13:11 and 12 Remember they were practicing religion but they were not following the express will and Word of God!

From day one, CHRIST had a difficult time in this sin-laden world. He being the hope of the world was in a challenging situation straight from the womb. **"And the dragon stood before the woman which was ready to be delivered, for to devour her Child as soon as it was born."** Rev. 12:4 Again, you know the story; if not, it is in your Bible. Read it! Herod was mocked by the wise men that did not return unto him upon his request. So in his desperation, he attempted to eliminate any hope of a newborn King and tried to kill baby JESUS by sending soldiers to destroy all the children of Bethlehem who were two years old and younger. This slaying of the innocents fulfilled the prophesy of Jeremiah Jer. 31:15, which said, **"In Rama was there a voice heard, lamentation, and weeping, and great mourning, Rachel weeping for her children, and would not be comforted, because they are not."** Matt. 2:18 Therefore this apostate king being used by the dragon made a futile attempt to eradicate the Savior of the world by killing innocent babies, but to the glory of God, it was of no avail.

An angel appeared to Joseph in a dream and told him to take the child with his mother and flee to Egypt. They were instructed to remain there until the death of Herod. **"That it might be fulfilled which was spoken of the LORD by the prophet, 'Out of Egypt have I called My Son.'"** Matt. 2:15 After the death of Herod, Joseph returned from Egypt unto his people with his young family to the city of Nazareth. **"And he came and dwelt in a city called Nazareth: that it might be fulfilled which was spoken by the prophets, 'He shall be called a Nazarene.'"** Matt. 2:23 Time and time again prophecy is seen to consistently being fulfilled.

JESUS grew up like most children and played in the streets of Nazareth. But at a very early age, He began to consider His purpose for being here in the test tube. On one occasion, He went to the temple with His parents and saw the priests offering the sacrificial lamb; He understood that the sacrifice was symbolic of Him. He could feel it in His bones. As one may feel the calling to become prophet or priest, Jesus looking upon this innocent victim giving his life as a substitute for the sinner, there was a strong sensation that came over Him. He knew without a doubt that this was His calling.

When Jesus was approximately twelve years old, His parents went to Jerusalem (the city of peace) to keep the Passover service, but when they were returning home, they discovered that their Son JESUS was not with them. Since there was a large crowd of them—friends and extended family (cousins, uncles, and aunts, etc.)—they thought that JESUS might be with one of them and went a whole day's journey before realizing that JESUS was not in their company. They returned back to Jerusalem to search for their beloved Son. When they arrived in the city, they searched everywhere for Him because it took them three days to find the young lad. It is imaginable that they looked everywhere back then where young folk might be found today. The sock hops, movie houses, jazzy skating rinks, discos, nightclubs for young people, arcade game rooms, street corners, sleepovers, everywhere but the church! Then I would imagine that after three days of searching in all the wrong places, they remembered what type of child and who the angels had proclaimed JESUS was! So they came to their senses and went to the temple and found Him there, exactly where you should be able to find your children today! In the church! The outcome of our children and the futuristic societal outlook would be a lot better off if more children of today could be, as Jesus, found in church! If parents would be more effective in directing their children to Jesus and to an uncorrupt church, then the spiritual outlook in society would not look so dismal! Jesus should be the example in all things even with our children. **"And it came to pass, that after three days they found Him in the temple, sitting in the mist of the doctors, both hearing them, and asking them questions. And all that heard Him were astonished at His understanding and answers."** Lk 2:46 and 47

Other than this incident at the temple when JESUS was about twelve years old sitting with the PhDs of His time, there is hardly anything else mentioned in the scriptures concerning His childhood or young adult life. We know that His earthly father's (Joseph's) trade was carpentry, and that it was common practice in their day for the father to make of their profession an apprentice of their sons. He was often called the carpenter's son. **"Is not this the carpenter's Son? Is not His mother called Mary? And His brethren, James, and Joses, and Simon, and Judas?"** Matt. 13:55

When JESUS was approximately thirty years old, scripture declares that He gave up His worldly profession and began His public ministry right here in the test tube. After His baptism in the Jordan River by John the Baptist, He received His anointing from on High which was beforehand prophesied by Isaiah and Daniel, the prophets of God. **"The Spirit of the Lord GOD is upon me; because the LORD hath <u>anointed</u> Me to preach good tidings unto the meek; He hath sent Me to bind up the** brokenhearted, to proclaim liberty to the captives, and the opening of the prison to them that are bound: To proclaim the acceptable year of the LORD, and the day of vengeance of our God; to comfort all that morn." Isa. 61:1 and 2 "Seventy weeks are determined upon thy people and upon thy holy city, to finish the transgression, and to make an end of sins, and to make reconciliation for iniquity, and to bring in everlasting righteousness, and to seal up the vision and prophecy, and to <u>anoint</u> the Most Holy." Dan. 9:24

After Jesus's baptism and anointing, He was led into the wilderness by the Spirit to be tried by the same arch deceiver that tempted Eve in the garden and the same devil that tempts you and me. Needless to say, Jesus passed every test! Amen! And He wants you and me to pass them too. JESUS realized that we are not as strong as Him and that many times we would have difficulty, but it is for this very reason why He came down here to show us the right way and to help us in our most difficult trails. Without forcing Himself on us, He would help us in every way that He could if we would allow Him to. He wants us to have the salvation that He has provided more than we want to accept it. Again, He will not force it on you. He gave his life as a sacrifice for our sins that when we are tried, as He was, and if we fail, which we do, we can have another chance through Him. Only through Jesus can we gain another chance to get it right and be endowed with light. Do not be fooled to think the power lies within yourself, your career, your bank account, the material goods built up, idols placed ahead of God, expensive cars, big houses, and your relationships; only in Christ Jesus can true peace and happiness be found.

Remember, JESUS begun His work with His own at Jerusalem (the church). Jesus, the Son of GOD, was also rejected and despised by His own (the church) at that time. Recall a similar rejection of Him took place in Samuel's day when they asked for a king to rule over them other than the true King of the universe. "Suppose ye that I am come to give peace on the earth? I tell you, Nay, but rather division." Lk 12:51

Jesus came, speaking peace, grace, truth, love, and salvation, but they would not have it! **"O Jerusalem, Jerusalem [*Israel-the church*] thou that killest the prophets and stonest them which are sent unto thee, how often would I have gather thy children together, even as a hen gather her chickens under her wings, and you would not! Behold, your house is left unto you desolate."** Matt. 23:37 and 38

Would the church today do any differently? They cast Him out then, and it is possible that He is being cast out today. The world so full of sin, reproach, hatred, and vice did not want to see or hear anything pure, true, and righteous. JESUS, the Son of the living GOD, often could not so much as preach or teach in His own house! **"He came unto His own, and His own received Him not."** Jn. 1:11

Often He had to preach and teach at places away from the walls of the temple and from the so-called leaders. He would be found down by the Sea of Galilee or on the Mount of Olives somewhere. But the thing to note is that He went on about His Father's business despite higher-arcs' opposition to Him and to His Father's will. He and John the Baptist both did not wait on ecclesiastical authorization to teach and to preach GOD's truths. They went about their Father's business without a PhD or any degree for that matter. They had a job related to the salvation of man to do, and they set out to do it. And guess what? They did it! They both ultimately paid with their lives the price of living a righteous life. Oftentimes, when an individual set out to do GOD's perfect will in this world, I guarantee that they will encounter opposition too! And further, the more *sincere* they are in doing God's will, the greater severity of the opposition will be imposed upon them. **"For if they do these things in a green tree, what shall be done in the dry?"** Lk. 23:31 This is the question JESUS posed to those that were diligently trying to follow Him as He was suffering for the sin of the world. He being the green tree, we being the dry and He spoke of things that would come to pass after His death. He told His followers not to weep for Him but to cry for themselves.

"But Jesus turning unto them said, 'Daughters of Jerusalem, weep not for me, but weep for yourselves, and for your children.'"LK23:28

At the precise time appointed, JESUS's adversaries finally caught up with HIM after He preached, taught, and demonstrated the way of life for three and a half years fulfilling all that was spoken of Him by the prophets. The inevitable had to come to pass and one of the last statements JESUS left to a perishing world was, "If you LOVE ME keep MY Commandments" Jn. 14:15 "This is MY Commandment that you LOVE one another as I have LOVED you." Jn. 15:12

The entire theme of GOD's creation and His plan of salvation hinges on unconditional *love* for you and me.

The part of our test-tube experience concerning CHRIST is all about love. And remember, there are only two parts you can be a part of. The other part is against all that Christ stands for. Now the question arises. Which one of the two are you for? The enemies of all righteousness, love, mercy, and truth came up against the Savior of the world. Again they rejected CHRIST and despised Him. Things were done to Him that He did not deserve. What was done to CHRIST was what should have been done to you and me. "He is despised and rejected of men; a man of sorrows and acquainted with grief: and we hid as it were our faces from Him; He was despised, and we esteemed Him not. Surely He hath borne our grief, and carried our sorrows: yet we did esteem Him stricken, smitten of GOD, and afflicted. But He was wounded for our transgressions; He was bruised for our iniquities: the chastisement of our peace was upon Him; and with His stripes we are healed. All we like sheep have gone astray; we have turned everyone to his own way; and the LORD hath laid on Him the iniquity of us all." Isa. 53:3–6

CHRIST the Savior of all mankind was taken out, ridiculed, beaten, spat upon, and finally nailed to a cross! All this, He did for you and me. "And I lay down My life for the sheep." Jn. 10:15

They thought that they were taking the life of JESUS and snuffing out the light of the world but He said that, **"No man taketh it from Me, but I lay it down of Myself. I have power to lay it down, and I have power to take it again. This commandment have I received of My Father."** Jn. 10:18 JESUS knew that He was the Lamb slain from the foundation of the world and that all prophecies had to be fulfilled. The scriptures cannot be broken, and even the precise time of JESUS's death was foretold. **"And when JESUS had cried with a loud voice, He said, 'Father into Thy hands I commend My Spirit:' and having said thus, He gave up the ghost."** Lk. 24:36

JESUS was born in a borrowed manger, and He was buried in a borrowed tomb, but He rose up from that grave King of Kings and Lord of Lords!

We have got to pause for a moment and contemplate on these things. Jesus came into this world viewed as a pauper. After His baptism by John the Baptist and anointing of the Holy Spirit by God the Father, Jesus began His work and ministry for the purpose of saving souls. He worked for exactly three and a half years and was crucified right on time as prophesied. Now the question poses itself for unbelievers. How in the world did Jesus pull off this immensely worldwide recognition if He was not the Son of the Living God? How could anyone born into a poor family (from a worldly perspective), work only three and a half years, had twelve men (not a corporation) working closely with Him, and finally be killed at the end of those three and a half years, and now at present be known globally better than any other single individual in history. He is known better than any poet, actor, singer, politician, dignitary, monarch, prelate, or any other single individual in the whole wide world?! Even most non-Christian religions have heard of Jesus but there are a lot of Christians who have never heard of the other religious spiritual leaders and even if they have, they may not know who they were or what they represented. The question is how did Jesus do this? THE SON OF GOD! That's how! **"For the earth shall be filed with the knowledge of the glory of the LORD, as the waters cover the sea."** Hab. 2:14

Jesus was nailed to the cross on the sixth day, that is the Day of Preparation. We recognize it today as Good Friday. **"And now when the even was come, because it was the preparation, that is, the day before the Sabbath, Joseph of Arimathaea, an honorable counselor, which also waited on the kingdom of GOD, came, and went in boldly unto Pilate, and crave the body of JESUS."** MK 15:42 and 43

The disciples and all those who followed JESUS went home to keep the Sabbath the day after the day of preparation. The seventh day, the Sabbath, was the only day between Good Friday (the day of preparation) the sixth day and the first day of the week (Easter Sunday), that is the day when our LORD and SAVIOR arose from the grave. The ladies would not even anoint His body until the Sabbath was past because they went home to keep GOD's Holy Day. **"And when the Sabbath was past, Mary Magdalene, and Mary the mother of James, and Salome, had brought sweet spices, that they might come and anoint Him."** Mk 16:1

They had seen two days before, that is the day before the Sabbath, where the men had laid JESUS. But when they arrived there at the grave site, they found that something interesting had happened. The heavy stone that they saw several men place over the tomb had miraculously been removed. **"And very early in the morning the first day of the week, they came unto the sepulcher at the rising of the sun. And they said among themselves, 'Who shall roll us away the stone from the door of the sepulcher?' And when they looked, they saw that the stone was rolled away: for it was very great."** Mk16:1-4 (How often are there before you great stones of circumstances in your life that needs removing by God?)

Now on that resurrection morning, when they entered the tomb expecting to see the body of JESUS laying there, He was not, for He had risen like He said. There was an angelic presence there at the tomb, and it was told to the ladies what had happened, and the angels were wondering why on earth they were seeking the living among the dead. I mean if you wanted ice cubes, the last place you would look for them is in an oven, would you? So then why were the ladies there at a grave site, a cemetery, a place for the dead looking for a living God? **"He is not here, but is risen: remember how He spake unto you when He was yet in Galilee? Saying, 'The Son of man must be delivered into the hands of sinful men, and be crucified, and on the third day rise again.'"** Lk 24:6 and 7

They were looking in the wrong place. He had told them that He would rise the third day and not be there in the tomb but because of not listening and a lack of faith, they did not hear Him.

Another point to bring to light is, unlike popular belief, where many people and theologians alike believe that the prophetic "three days and three nights" prophecy began at Jesus's death. They believe that when Jesus spoke of spending three days and three nights in the heart of the earth, that He was referring to the tomb. Not so my friends, if you take careful note of the text of Luke 24:7 **"The Son of man *must* be delivered into the hands of sinful men, and be crucified, and on the third day rise again"**. (Several texts could be used here, but Luke 24:7 was the one selected.) If you noticed, this prophecy begins to be fulfilled the night Jesus was betrayed by Judas Iscariot and precisely at the point when they laid their sinful hands on Him. The key word that causes this prophecy's cohesiveness is the conjunction *and*. **"And in the *evening* He cometh with the twelve. And as they sat and did eat Jesus said, 'Verily I say unto you, one of you which eateth with me shall betray me'."** Mk 14:17 and 18 **"And immediately, while He yet spake, cometh Judas, one of the twelve, and with him a great multitude with swords and staves, from the chief priests and the scribes and the elders . . . And they laid their hands on Him, and took Him."** Mk 14:43 and 46 This event took place on a Thursday night according to man's alteration of time; however; if we look at it by God's sequencing of days, it was Friday evening. [This is based on God's pattern of days during creation in the book of Genesis. The pattern of evening and morning constituting a complete day, (notice the creation week of Genesis 1. Every day of creation begins with evening and ends with morning. Thus evening and morning were the first day, the second day, the third day, and etc.) Not by man's standard of morning being the first part and evening the second part of a day as we perceive it to be today.] For the rest of that night, Jesus was before the leaders and continued until the next morning being accused falsely. **"And straightway in the *morning* the chief priests held a consultation with the elders and scribes and the whole council, and bound Jesus, and carried Him away, and delivered Him to Pilate . . . *And* as Pilate, willing to content the people, released Barabbas unto them, and delivered Jesus; when he had scourged Him, to be crucified . . . *And* it was the third hour, and they crucified Him."** Mk 15:1, 15 and 25 That constitutes one full day of Friday, the sixth day. It is now **one complete evening and morning.** Thursday night, they laid their hands on Him and held a fake trial. The next morning, He was bound and taken to Pilate. All day, Pilate tried to find some way to release Jesus due to a dream his wife had the night before. Pilate, however, attempting to appease the people, released Barabbas, a murderer, to them and sentenced Jesus to be scourged and crucified. Now it is sunset Friday and the beginning of the second night Jesus is in the heart of the earth. **"Now when *even* was come, because it was the preparation, that is the day before the Sabbath. Joseph of Armiathaea, an honorable counselor, which also waited for the kingdom of God, came and went in boldly unto Pilate, and craved the body of Jesus."** Mk 15:42 and 43 **"Now from the sixth hour there was darkness over all the land unto the ninth hour . . . And about the ninth hour Jesus cried with a loud voice, saying, Eli, Eli, la-ma sa-bach-tha-ni? That is to say, My God, My God, why hast thou forsaken Me?"** Matt. 27:45 and 46 **"And that day was the preparation and the Sabbath drew on . . . And the women returned, and prepared spices and ointments; and rested the Sabbath day according to the commandment."** Lk 23:54–56

Again, this begins the second evening or night of Jesus's ordeal and the second night the prophecy is being fulfilled. It is also when the Sabbath begun. It was Sabbath evening (Friday night as we know it today) when Jesus, the Son of God, was laid in the tomb. The evening passed then the second part of the Sabbath (the morning) came and past. The Sabbath drew on the Bible says and Jesus continued to lay there in the tomb. Now two complete days and nights of the prophecy are past. In order to complete the prophecy, Christ had to stay there in the tomb another night and at least some part of another morning to complete the prophetic three days and three nights. The night after Sabbath is the evening of the first day of the week. We call it Saturday night, but according to the Bible, it is actually Sunday evening (night). This night also passes with our Savior still resting in the tomb as He said.

The second part of the third day is approaching. Faint rays of light are beginning to peek over the horizon. A powerful angel is sent by God the Father to awaken our Lord, "Thy Father calleth Thee!" The stone was rolled away, and the guard of soldiers fell asleep as dead men. Very early on the third morning of the prophesy on the first day of the week, the Bible tells us, Jesus got up and walked out of the tomb just like He said He would! Hallelujah!! **"And when *Sabbath was past*, Mary Magdalene, and Mary the mother of James, and Salome, had bought sweet spices, that they might come and anoint Him."** Mk 16: **"And very early in the morning the first day of the week, they came unto the sepulcher at the rising of the sun."** Mk 16:2 Think about this miraculous event for a moment. While Christ walked the earth, He healed and brought many folk back to life from death but think about He Himself laying there in the tomb a lifeless form. All of a sudden, breathe, and the spirit of life returns unto His body. He rises up from His resting place all on His own! Just maybe, this is a physical indication of how the spirit of life and the highest wisdom came together at the birth of divinity and raised Himself up before the universe was! (Just food for thought; speak your mind.)

This in essence completes the prophetic three days and three nights Jesus was to be in the belly of the earth as Jonah was three days and three nights in the belly of the whale. Again, to be clear, it begun that Thursday night when sinful men laid hands on Christ and did to Him as they listed. Christ was crucified on the sixth day, the day then known as day of preparation; that is the day before the Sabbath. Further evidence of this is the fact that today we call this day Good Friday. Christ rose very early in the morning on the first day of the week at the rising of the sun. The day of His resurrection on the first day of the week, the name of Easter Sunday has been applied.

Now notice, the only full day (evening and morning) between the sixth day when He was crucified and the first day of the week when He arose is the only complete full evening and morning of the three-day prophecy that Jesus rested in the tomb which was the seventh day, and it was the Sabbath day. **"Remember the Sabbath Day to keep it Holy."** Ex. 20:8 This seventh day Sabbath just happens to be called Saturday in English.

After His resurrection, CHRIST was seen by His apostles, but to authenticate His ascension into heaven, it was witnessed by some of His followers. **"And when He had spoken these things, while they beheld, He was taken up; and a cloud received Him out of their sight. And while they looked steadfastly toward heaven as he went up, behold two men stood by them in white apparel; which also said, 'Ye men of Galilee, why stand ye gazing up into heaven? This same JESUS, which is taken up from you into heaven, shall so come in like manner as ye have seen Him go into heaven."** Acts 1:9–11

The Savior of the world ministry within the test tube had come to a conclusion. He had now ascended to the heavenly sanctuary to perform His ministerial function in heaven, fulfilling His priestly work in behalf of you and me. **"For CHRIST is not entered into the holy places made with hands, which are the figures of the true; but into heaven itself, now to appear in the presence of GOD for us."** Heb. 9:24

As when GOD came down and revealed Himself to the children of Israel when He delivered them out of Egypt and left it to them to spread His message of truth to the rest of a perishing world, so it was when CHRIST came down to deliver us (spiritual children of Israel) out of spiritual Egypt and out of spiritual bondage (worldliness). He left it to the Christian Church to carry the good news gospel to the rest of the world and to the ends of the earth. GOD is the same yesterday, today, and forever. Amen? JESUS told the church, **"Go ye therefore, and teach all nations, baptizing them in the name of the Father, the Son, and the Holy Spirit: Teaching them to observe all things whatsoever I have commanded you: and, lo, I am with you always, even unto the end of the world. Amen."** Matt. 28:19 and 20

experiment .
Christians may throughout
from the ... of the world as
of Israel to be a peculiar treasure ... the
people in the earth. Also he ... distinct and
godly deportment represent ... as ... this
"That ye are a chosen gen ...
peculiar ... tha ...
called you

THE EARLY CHRISTIAN CHURCH

After CHRIST's ascension, His followers were physically left behind here within the test tube but were admonished to continue the gospel work and all who would follow Him the promise was given that He would be with them spiritually even until the end of time. So keep in mind that tough Jesus left us physically, whenever we are in trouble, sick, or at any time in need of help He is with us Spiritually by way of The Comforter which He sent. **"Teach them to observe all things whatsoever I have commanded you: and lo, I am with you always, even unto the end of the world. Amen."** Matt. 28:20

Christ's followers loved Him and missed Him dearly. There were eleven of His twelve apostles (minus one, because Judas had hung himself) left behind to be the human factor used and directed by the HOLY SPIRIT, as the main thrust to propel the gospel truth to every nation of the world. These apostles were together waiting in the upper room for the promise of the Holy Spirit that would be poured out among them. **"And, being assembled together with them, commanded them that they should not depart from Jerusalem, but wait for the promise of the Father, which, saith He, 'Ye have heard of me…For John Truly baptized with water, but ye shall be baptized with the Holy Ghost not many days hence'."** Acts 1:4 and 5

There were also other disciples hanging out with the apostles numbered of one hundred and twenty, not to mention the women who were with them also. Another apostle was selected from the hundred and twenty disciples present to remake the original number of twelve. The total number of disciples gathered there were still one hundred and thirty one (120 + 11 = 131). After careful prayer, Matthias was selected to replace Judas. Keep in mind that the message was first given to the ones who were first to do the work. GOD wanted so badly for the children of Israel as a nation to fulfill the promise HE had made with Abraham, even after the death of HIS dear SON on Calvary's Cross. **"Ye are the children of the prophets, and of the covenant which GOD made with our fathers, saying unto Abraham, 'And to thy seed shall all the kindred's of the earth be blessed.' Unto you first GOD, having raised up His Son JESUS, sent Him to bless you, in turning away every one of you from his iniquities."** Acts 3:25 **namely the Jewish nation the children of the promise (Israel).**

When the Syrophenician woman was requesting that JESUS would cast out the demon from her daughter, Jesus told her that the blessings must first be given to the children of the promise. **"But JESUS said unto her, 'Let the children first be filled."** Mk. 7:27 The gospel was for the whole world, but GOD wanted Israel to be a peculiar treasure and a nation of priests dispensing His saving grace by His Word to every corner of the globe. **"Now therefore if you will obey My voice indeed, and keep My covenant, then ye shall be a peculiar treasure unto Me above <u>all</u> people: for all the earth is Mine: And ye shall be unto Me a kingdom of priests, and an Holy nation."** Ex. 19:5 and 6

The requirements today are the same; they have not changed for contemporary Christians. God has not changed; He still requires His children to be a peculiar treasure of priesthood and not be conformed to this world. So were the early Christians, and so it should be today with later-day Christians. **"Who gave himself for us, that He might redeem us from all iniquity, and purify unto Himself a peculiar people, zealous of good works."** Ti. 2:14

Christians today should not attempt to be like the rest of the world but to be noticeably different, taking on a different and distinct godly disposition in Christ. **"But ye are a chosen generation, a royal priesthood, and holy nation, a peculiar people, that ye should show forth the praises of Him who hath called you out of darkness into His marvelous light."** 1 Pet. 2:9 Again, even when CHRIST came He tried to reinitiate the promise to the children but as a nation they would not have it. They faltered at the beginning, and they faltered at the end. Hopefully, this is not the case with the so-called Christian churches today. However, it begs the question: Are today's self-proclaimed Christians moving along in a westwardly fashion in a straight line? Are the same principles being followed as the early church? Or are similar practices taking place as did Ancient Israel when they constantly strayed away from GOD's precepts and taught for doctrines the precepts of men? **"HE answered and said unto them, 'Well hath Esaias prophesied of you hypocrites as it is written, This people honoureth me with their lips, but their heart is *far* from me. Howbeit in vain do they worship ME, teaching for doctrines the commandments of men.'"** Mk. 7:6 and 7 Is every Christian the same as CHRIST? But before you start to look around, look within first! The very definition of Christian is one who is CHRIST-like or one whose day-to-day behavior is that of CHRIST's, or has the contemporary Christian deviated from the standard by some unperceived measurable degree. Are there watered-down Christians today? Are today's churches off spiritual course and are not aware of it? These and similar questions need to be faithfully addressed by Christian members and clergy alike if Jesus is to be seen in the beauty of His Holiness by all who claim to seek His face.

Applying a scientific analogy to this point of view: In trigonometry (the study of angles), if your angle of coordinates or tangent is off by a small margin, the farther away you get from the originating point, the more off course you will be. In other words, as time increases, the amount of distance increases of being off course, that is, if the speed remains constant. For example, if you were on a ship leaving from the northeastern coast of America at New York Harbor and heading for the northwest coast of Africa, say to Morocco, and if the angle is off at the point of origin by only a small fraction and you continue going forward in a straight line, it is possible for you to end up in Europe. Simply because the angle of departure was off by a small margin, the end results can be devastating. You can end up somewhere you did not intend to go. The same is true for the off course church or Christian! If not careful they can miss heaven and end up somewhere else! If either gets off course at any point during the pilgrim's journey, the end results could and will be spiritually devastating. That is, if correcting maneuvers are not taken to get the ship or the individual life back on course.

In order to regain bearings and to get back on the correct course, there must first be a recognition that you are indeed off course. If there is no recognition, then it is virtually impossible to get back on course and regain correct living in Christ. This can be somewhat difficult to do because it is easy to get comfortable with the newfound direction and once you begin to gather a head of steam in the wrong direction, it is all the more difficult to take corrective action to get back on the right track. **"Thus saith the LORD, 'Stand ye in the ways, and see, and ask for the old paths, where is the good way, and walk therein, and ye shall find rest for your souls'. But they said, 'We will not walk therein.'"** Jer. 6:16 They will not walk therein because they find it easier to continue in the wrong direction or on the downward path.

It is more so the captain's or leader's responsibility to turn the ship (the church) or your personal ship (the individual) around to get back on the right course of God through Jesus Christ.

The contemporary Christian Church (the main ship or collective body) has been plodding along through uncharted waters since the Dark Ages. And it's frightening to think that due to the human error factor and the enemy's (the devil's) relentless torpedo fire at the ship (deception and vice), there is a high probability that the ship is at best off course and at worst rapidly sinking. **"For the mystery of iniquity doth already work."** 2 Thess. 2:7

Make no mistake; GOD's true church will make it into its final destination. The faithful few, who are seeking to do GOD's perfect will, will undoubtedly make it in. Considering the individual, **"Be ye therefore perfect, even as your Father which is in Heaven is perfect."** Matt. 5:48 these collectively will make up the end church. Considering the church, **"That He might present it to Himself a glorious church, not having spot, or wrinkle, or any such thing; but that it should be holy and without blemish."** Eph. 5:27

The individuals that are God's people should be seeking perfection in Christ so as to make up the body of Christ, which is His church. He is coming back for as the scriptures testify for a church, "without spot or wrinkle." In this instance, Christ has likened His church to a pure and clean garment. If you were going to a very important meeting or to a formal dinner party, you would not wear a suit or dress with noticeable spots or wrinkles in it, would you? The answer to this question is no! Neither does Jesus want spots and wrinkles in His people! **"Then said Jesus unto His disciples, 'If any man will come after Me, let him deny himself, and take up his cross, and follow Me. For whosoever will save his life shall lose it: and whosoever will lose his life for My sake shall find it.'"** Matt. 16:24–25

During the Dark Ages, millions of true Christians were martyred and killed for the truth's sake. These people who sought out God's perfection in their daily lives will be part of the true ship (God's church) that Jesus is coming back to receive unto Himself at the end of time. A good biblical example of this can be viewed from a spiritual perspective when Paul was as a prisoner and was being sent to Rome on a ship. The ship was lost and sunk, but the apostle Paul still made it in and all those who believed his words. **"But after long abstinence Paul stood forth in the midst of them, and said, 'Sirs, ye should have hearkened unto me, and not have loosed from Crete, and to have gained this harm and loss. And now I exhort you to be** of good cheer: for there shall be no loss of any man's life among you, but of the ship.'"Act27:21and22 Paul did not waver because the ship's captain did not follow a straight "Thus saith the LORD!" He kept right on believing and did not lower the standards one bit. Often today, many get sidetracked and off course because they followed a self-seeking non-Christian leader as opposed to following the leader as he follows Christ. When the leader ceases to follow a straight message then it is time to part the waves. **"Paul admonished them, and said unto them, 'Sirs, I perceive that this voyage will be with hurt and much damage, not only of the lading and ship but also our lives.' Nevertheless, the centurion believed the master and owner of the ship, more than those things which were spoken by Paul."** Acts 27:9–11 It is of necessity to say that so often today's ships (the present-day churches) go off course because leaders or captains of churches listen to men rather than GOD. **"You hypocrites, well did Esaias prophesy of you saying, 'This people draw nigh unto me with their mouth and honor me with their lips; but their heart is far from me. But in vain they do worship me teaching for doctrines the commandments of men."** Matt. 15:7–9

Not long after Paul had given them the instructions from God, there arose against the ship a very tempestuous wind called Euroclydon (read Acts 27). After telling them what was going to happen and when they did not listen, Paul did not rush in to say, "I told you so." The Bible says, **"But after long abstinence Paul stood forth in the midst of them, and said, 'Sirs, ye should of harken unto me, and not have loosed from Crete, and to have gain this harm and loss."** Acts 27:21

Leaders today should harken and listen to the voice of the prophets. Both past and present! The apostle Paul goes on to tell us that the ship went on to sink (Read it in your Bible, Acts 27). This is exactly why at this point in time, true unwavering Christians should not be looking around at others but taking a closer look at the true reference point. That is, while Jesus walked the earth (how He conducted Himself and right after His ascension), the early church (how they treated one another and lived). This is as close as we are going to get as to the true conduct of the individual and the church as a whole and how we should perform or conduct ourselves in service and worship to God. Using some reference point other than the early church in the book of Acts, may be well off course already before you even take the reference.

If a sample were to be tested within some scientific discipline, you would almost always have to (more times than not) use some form of reference by which everything else is tested. A standard would be established. As for a standard concerning today's contemporary churches, the early church should be referenced to see how it should operate as a unit body, continuing on a straight path until Jesus is seen coming back in the clouds of glory. Not deviating from the concepts, standards, and principles that the early church and the apostles practiced. That is loving one another, communing with one another, fellowshipping with one another, and being on one accord is very necessary for contemporary Christians.

CHRIST told His followers (the members of the early church) to wait at Jerusalem until they received power from on high. If they had attempted to carry on the work without this power from on high, it would not have been successful. They needed this power to go forward with the everlasting gospel. **"But ye shall receive power, after that the HOLY SPIRIT is come upon you: and ye shall be witnesses unto Me both in Jerusalem, and in all Judaea, and in Samaria, and unto the uttermost parts of the earth."** Acts 1:8

The disciples were instructed to wait until they heard from GOD, not so today. Today you might hear, "Go to college or a theological institute and get a degree from man so that you can receive power to preach the Word!" It is fearful to think of the possibility that most ministers coming out of the universities today are empowered by man and not God. Simply because they may be eloquent orators and can speak and teach smooth things or because they have a popular name these are often used as criteria to become a leader of God's church! **"Which say to the seers, See not; and to the prophets, prophesy not unto us right things, speak unto us smooth things, prophesy deceits."** Isa. 30:10 Paul wrote, **"And He gave some, apostles; and some, prophets; and some, evangelists; and some, pastors and teachers; for the perfecting of the saints, for the work of the ministry, for the edifying of the body of CHRIST."** Eph. 4:11 and 12 Where does it say He gave some a degree or a certificate? That you needed to be a graduate from a theological seminary before you can truly understand and interpret GOD's word? Where does it say that? Not to mention one going out to teach in Jesus' name. To which seminary did John the Baptist go? **"Wherefore the LORD said, 'Forasmuch as this people draw near unto Me with their mouth, and with their lips do honour Me, but have removed their heart far from Me, and their fear [*respect*] toward Me is taught by the <u>precept of men</u>.'"** Isa. 29:13

By some man-made organized standards, it seems almost as if you cannot get near a pulpit to teach and to preach unless you have a PhD and the ability to arouse sensational emotionalism. Somebody somewhere is going to be held accountable for these fallacies. **"Howbeit in vain do they worship me, teaching for doctrines the commandments of men."** Mk 7:7

Early Christians were on one accord and prayerfully waiting for the promise that their LORD and Savior would send them power from on high. For all those seeking to do God's will, latter Christians should be doing the same!

The Comforter (Holy Spirit) came down upon them so mightily that it appeared as if tongues of fire were resting upon them and they began to speak in other languages. The power of God was so strong and the urgent need for His message to go forth with power; He had given them the ability to preach to foreigners in their own language, and not one of them had to go get a degree in a foreign language. Why? Because they were empowered from on high! "**And when the day of Pentecost was fully come, they were all with one accord in one place . . . And suddenly there came a sound from heaven as of a rushing mighty wind, and it filled all the house where they were sitting . . . And there appeared unto them cloven tongues like as of fire, and it sat upon each of them . . . And they were all filled with the Holy Ghost, and began to speak with other tongues, as the Spirit gave them utterance."** Acts 2:1–4

Really ponder and consider what happened that day on the Day of Pentecost. That was a spectacular and momentous sight to behold. To actually witness the power of God coming down like that upon men. And to hear people of different nationalities receiving the gospel in their own languages being preached by unlearned men! As a matter of fact, it was thought by some that they had been drinking all morning and had become drunk! They were drunk all right but not by liquor. They were doused by double shots of the HOLY SPIRIT to preach the truth. Amen. They were indeed taught by the SPIRIT of GOD and received their theological training from on high. **"Others mocking said, 'These men are full of new wine.'"** Acts 2:13

Contrary to some popular beliefs that the apostles were speaking in some unknown utterances that no one could understand, it needs to be specified that the tongues here meant as it clearly states that they were speaking in another language. They were not babbling, and they were not speaking in some strange unknown mysterious garble. They did not have to go to college to learn Greek if they could not speak Greek. The HOLY SPIRIT provided the power from on high if one needed to speak the language of the people needing witnessing to. **"And there were dwelling at Jerusalem Jews, devout men, out of every nation under heaven. Now when this was noised abroad, the multitude came together, and was confounded, because that every man heard them speak in his own <u>language</u>."** Acts 2:5 and 6

The WORD of GOD points out clearly that the unknown tongue was without question another language and not some utterance that no man could understand. In other words, if people were there from the land of Greece, there was at least one apostle there speaking a straight thus saith the Lord and the goodness of God in Greek. He would speak in Greek, and someone there could interpret what the Spirit was saying in Greek. On the other hand, if He was speaking in Greek, what good would that be if no one there could speak Greek? It would be an unfruitful waste of time, and that is not characteristic of God. **"Wherefore let him that speaketh in an unknown tongue** [language] **pray that he may interpret. For if I pray in an unknown tongue, my spirit prayeth, but my understanding is unfruitful. What is it then? I will pray with the spirit, and I will pray with the understanding also: I will sing with the spirit, and I will sing with the understanding also. Else when thou shalt bless with the spirit, how shall he that occupieth the room of the unlearned say Amen at the giving of thanks, seeing he understandeth not what thou sayest?"** 1 Cor. 14:13–16 In other words if someone was truly preaching in Greek if there was no one there who could speak Greek then the person speaking in the unknown language of Greek would appear to be rambling and there would be confusion. No one there can say amen because there would be no understanding. Every country represented there at Jerusalem by the upper room on the day of Pentecost heard the gospel of Jesus preached in their own language (tongue) spoken by at least one of the twelve apostles and they could understand therefore they could say amen.

Instead of those men recognizing the power of GOD and giving all praises due Him they marveled at the men who were from Galilee (mostly fishermen or so) speaking many different languages of other countries when they had not been learned at the university. They were more awed by the gift of the Spirit in the men instead of listening to what the Spirit of God was attempting to express to them by way of the men. Are the same attitudes being displayed within the popular churches of today? Praising, glorifying, and acknowledging men for their works and deeds at times when GOD and only GOD should be acknowledged and glorified! Intense glorification of men during the worship services! When it should be in fact GOD and only GOD who receives the praise, honor, and glory? **"And they were all amazed and marveled, saying one to another, 'Behold, are not all these which speak Galileans? And how hear we every man in our own tongue [*language*], wherein we were born?'"** Acts 2:7 and 8 **"And they were all <u>amazed</u>, and were in doubt, saying one to another, 'What meaneth this?' Others mocking said, 'These men are full of new wine.'"** Acts 2:12 and 13 Again, these men were not drunk but represented the fulfillment of the promise to receive power from on high. The only reason they spoke in another language (tongue) was for the express purpose of spreading the Gospel of Jesus Christ. There was no other reason. It was not to show off that they were endowed by the Spirit, nor was it to prove to anyone that they were of the Spirit. They were preaching the WORD! That's it!

Most of the disciples of CHIRST went about doing exactly as CHRIST had commissioned them to do. Please keep in mind, however, that as Judas was, so is not everyone claiming to be a Christian is a Christian. So these apostles were not only speaking eloquently with power, but they were speaking other languages being unlearned. There were, however, people of the opposition who had been to the university and thought they knew everything and these unlearned men should not be out there doing the LORD's work at all. After all, "who authorized them to teach and preach in the name of the Lord?" Some of the leaders and scholars of the day felt like they were GOD's gift to mankind and if GOD did not come through them, then obviously there had to have been some type of mistake. In other words, how in the world are these unlearned men out here preaching to us and telling us what's going on with God when they have not been to our schools?

A good example is when Peter and John were about to enter the temple at the gate called Beautiful. There they healed a lame man in the name of JESUS. The people marveled at Peter and John as if by their own power they did these things. So Peter began to preach to them and explain to them the goodness of GOD by way of the HOLY SPIRIT. But there were some who were thought to be church folk there. **"And it came to pass on the morrow, that their rulers, and elders, and scribes, and Annas the high priest, and Caiaphas, and John, and Alexander, and as many as were of the kindred of the high priest, were gather together at Jerusalem. And when they had set them [Peter and John] in the midst, they asked, 'By what power [*authority*], or by what name, have ye done this?'"** Acts 4:6 and 7

That is by whose authority or permission did they heal the afflicted. "They did not come to us!" they shouted.

Because many of the followers of JESUS did not have an education, some of the leaders felt that these unlearned men were not smart enough to follow GOD and receive His SPIRIT to discern spiritual things. JESUS healed a man that had been blind from his birth and some of the then-known church leaders did not believe in CHRIST and called this man before them to wit, who it was that healed him that was born blind. **"Then said they to him again, 'What did He to thee? How opened He thine eyes?' He answered them, 'I have told you already, and ye did not hear: wherefore would ye hear it again? Will ye also be His disciples?'"** Jn. 9:26 and 27 The leaders questioning him who had received his sight from JESUS continued on, **"Now we know that GOD hears not sinners: but if any man be a worshipper of GOD and doeth His will, him He heareth."** Jn. 9:31 They said the right thing to the blind man but they practiced not what they preached. For Jesus said, **"All therefore whatsoever they bid you observe, that observe and do; but do not ye after their works: for they say, and do not."** Matt. 23:3 Nevertheless, the healed man replied, **"'Since the world began was it not heard that any man opened the eyes of one that was born blind. If this man were not of GOD, He could do nothing.' They answered and said unto him, 'Thou** was altogether born in sins, and dost thou teach us?' And they cast him out." Jn. 9:32–34

This man was full of the SPIRIT of GOD. He had just had a lifesaving experience with JESUS, but he could not relate to these church leaders about the glory and power of God! They did not want to hear him. "He doesn't know anything—he hasn't been to our schools! Kick him out!" they cried. This seems to be the same spirit that asked JESUS, "By what authority do you cast out devils?" Again when the apostle Paul stood before the inquisition in Rome and when Martin Luther stood before the Diet at Worms, "By whose authority do you do these things?" Careful insight and consideration needs to be displayed by the leaders of today, so as they also do not fall to this same spirit of condemnation. All need to be careful, but special care needs to be exercised if in a leadership role to be mindful of the course of actions taken and the ability to discern those of a lower degree or stature in life. Not behaving harshly, nor possess a controlling spirit attempting to dictate to the conscience of men. They will have to give an account of every single soul encountered. The only name under heaven by which any of us can be saved is JESUS. "Neither is there salvation in any other: for there is none other name under heaven given among men, whereby we must be saved." Acts 4:12

"Now when they saw the boldness of Peter and John, and perceived that they were unlearned and ignorant men, they marveled; and they took knowledge of them, that they had been with JESUS." Acts 4:12 and 13

When you are truly following CHRIST, people will know it! They will be able to look at you, your disposition, and the way you do things. They will know that you spend time with Jesus and that you are different. Dear Christians, it is important that you continue your walk with CHRIST and do His will no matter who gets in your way. Walk the good walk and fight the good fight of faith regardless of what oppositions arise before, behind, or on every side of you. There is a true balance in heaven and a true measure of weight. The record is accurate. There are no flaws or mistakes in the heavenly record books. Everyone will ultimately give an account for whatsoever they say and do. So please do not get discouraged or bent out of shape for doing what is right! Just keep pressing forward in righteousness. Remember that they did the same thing to our LORD and SAVIOR JESUS CHRIST and to all the holy men of GOD which were before you. **"Blessed are they which are persecuted for righteousness' sake: for theirs is the kingdom of heaven. Blessed are ye, when men shall revile you, and persecute you, and shall say all manner of evil against you falsely, for My sake."** Matt. 5:10 and 11 JESUS continues to say, **"Rejoice and be exceeding glad; for great is your reward in heaven: for so persecuted they the prophets which were before you."** Matt. 5:12

JESUS, by way of the HOLY SPIRIT, is the one that authorizes all men to be in His service and it is Him that we must give an account to, not men. Of course, GOD gives certain men leadership talents and as long as those men are following CHRIST to edify the church in the correct fashion, then all those who are under their guidance should follow their lead. However, the moment the leader begins concentrating and focusing on self and starts deviating from following the LORD and SAVIOR, it is time for the followers of CHRIST to stop following the so-called leader and part the waves.

Compared to all the inhabitants of the entire world, there were only a humble few sincerely waiting for the promise of our LORD. They were encapsulated by this sin, sick, and wicked world while they waited. World affairs and the vicissitudes of daily life were hammering them on every side. Most people outside of this small group, much like most people today, probably thought that they knew everything and had all the answers. Much to their futile efforts, the leaders of that day attempted to quench the SPIRIT and halt the very work of GOD. They also believed that they were the guardians of the truth, when in actuality it was they who were preventing the Lord's work in the name of GOD. This is what makes this type of effort so deadly. They were blaspheming the HOLY SPIRIT by denouncing those who came by the Spirit proclaiming the true Messiah's Gospel and thought that they were doing GOD a favor by denouncing God's messengers. **"Wherefore I say unto you, all manner of sin and blasphemy shall be forgiven unto men: but the blasphemy against the HOLY GHOST shall not be forgiven unto men."** Matt. 12:31

This includes making unholy utterances or committing unholy acts against the HOLY SPIRIT, the spirit of righteousness. Today's leaders need to be *extra* careful that the same ungodly spirit does not creep into them, preventing those sent by God Himself because those sent may not have gone to their particular institution or dogmatized in their particular belief. Prayerful consideration must be given along with harmonizing the message with the word of God! If not, an account will have to be given to the Higher Power from which the message was sent. **"And when they had brought them, they set them before the council:** [*or the board, if a modern day church*] **and the high priest** [*organizational leader, president, or pastor*] **asked them, saying, 'Did not we straightly command you that ye should not teach in this name? And, behold, ye have filled Jerusalem with your doctrine, and intend to bring this man's blood upon us.'"** Acts 5:27 and 28

The apostles' courage was too strong for these antagonistically hypocritical leaders of the then-known church! **"Then Peter and the other apostles answered and said, 'We ought to obey <u>GOD</u> rather than men'."** Acts 5:29

Remember that the Christian Church within the test tube was in its purest form during the time of CHRIST's ministry and His resurrection. It needs to be noted that the recognizable church (they governing the temple) were in apostasy. They thought that they were the true church, though they did not heed the message that Messiah had come. The *true* Christian Church, on the other hand, was in that day following Jesus sometimes unnoticeably, and often this is the case today as well. Emphasis needs to be placed on the TRUTH simply because a Christian claim is made does not make it so!

The Anti-CHRIST had long been trying to disrupt and to distort GOD's truth and His plan. Is there any reason to think that he would take a break at this point in time? Not hardly, and as a matter of fact, he would and has stepped up his deceptive vices to try to counter the work. As the apostle Paul puts it, **"For the mystery of iniquity doth already work:"** 2 Thess. 2:7 If the enemy of all righteousness was already working in the early Christian Church to manipulate and to discourse the ship, it is only imaginable where he is within the ship today. For all who want a more meaningful, spiritual, and a closer walk with the *Lord* (not with men), please take a closer look in Acts chapter 2 at how the early Christian Church operated in their day. This is the key. Then use that as a reference point and compare it with the church of where you are today in an attempt to see if you and your church are still on course individually as well as collectively. **ONLY BY OBSERVATION OF THE ACCEPTABLE BIBLICALLY DESCRIPTIVE PRINCIPLES OF THE EARLY CHURCH CAN TODAY'S CHURCHES REFERENCE THEMSELEVES!**

There must be an immediate call for Revival and Reformation by any individual or church if not following the patterns of the true church outlined in Acts. It follows then, if a church group needs to get back on course, this simply acknowledges the fact that they are indeed off course to begin with. The onset of true spiritual healing always begins with the first step of recognition. That is, there is a need for change. In order for there to be a collective change, typically, the leaders are the ones who must receive this revelation for the need of change and a need to get back on the correct course to do what is right in the sight of an Almighty GOD. Otherwise, change for corrective actions would not take place. The members do not have the earthly authority to make a collective change of the ship, and usually they follow the pastor's queues and directions. Individuals are responsible for themselves. As concerning Paul, if the ship wants to sink that does not mean that you have to go down with it. Any and all souls lost due to unscriptural and unsound leadership will also fall on the leader that led people on a wrong course. Most times when the leaders see a need for change and begin taking measures to correct them, the common people will follow. Otherwise, the revival or the change hardly ever will take effect. It does not matter if the church appears to be doing well in certain areas such as finances for instance; there's a good possibility for the need of spiritual revival. Also, financial gain and economic well-being is not necessarily an indication that a ship is on the right course either. In fact, Jesus says, **"Because thou sayest, I am rich, and increased with goods, and have need of nothing; and knowest not that thou art wretched, and miserable, and poor, and blind, and naked."** Rev. 3:17 Jesus goes on to say, **"I counsel thee to buy of Me gold tried in the fire, that thou mayest be rich; and white raiment, that thou mayest be clothed, and that the shame of thy nakedness do not appear; and anoint thine eyes with eye salve, that thou mayest see."** Rev. 3:18 These texts apply to the individual or to an entire congregation as well for consideration of spiritual cleansing.

The first step in growth toward CHRIST is to recognize that there is a need for humility, a need for repentance, and a need for change. Whether it is for an individual, a church congregation, or an entire Christian organization, the need is almost always to get back on the straight paths. As Jeremiah puts it like this, **"Thus saith the Lord, 'Stand ye in the ways, and see, and ask for the old paths, where is the good way, and walk therein, _and ye shall find rest for your souls._' But they said, 'We will not walk therein.'."** Jer. 6:16 Jesus said something similar in the New Testament comparable to what Jeremiah was given by God the Father to say in the Old. **"Come unto Me, all ye that labour and are heavy laden, and I will give you rest. Take my yoke upon you and learn of Me, for I am meek and lowly in heart; _and ye shall find rest unto your souls._ For My yoke is easy and My burden is light."** Matt. 11:28–30 _Finding rest for your soul_ involves following a straight, 'Thus saith the Lord!' and that is following Christ, the straight Word of God made flesh. They are indeed one and the same. **"For I am persuaded, that neither death,** nor life, nor angels, nor principalities, nor powers, nor things present, nor things to come, nor height, nor depth, nor any other creature, shall be able to separate us from the love of God, which is in Christ Jesus our Lord."Act8:38and39

Let's put the early church under the microscope to observe what exactly took place with them during their test tube experiences soon after the resurrection and ascension of Jesus. Special care needs to be taken while observing exactly how they operated. Focus your eye and take a closer look at how they treated one another. Notice how much love was displayed. In order to do this, you must go to the WORD of God. The book of Acts especially in the first few chapters give a pretty good description of what took place after the brethren received power from on high.

Remember that at first, the eleven apostles, along with the women were in the upper room at Jerusalem. Again, there was another group of one hundred and twenty disciples or followers of Christ hanging around also. After the SPIRIT of GOD came down upon the apostles, they began to speak in other languages. Men from all different nationalities begin to flock to the scene because they could hear the wonderful news of the gospel in their own languages. The Bible says in the book of Acts that about *three thousand souls* were baptized that day. Hence, the dawning of the early Christian Church as we know it. The church in its infancy after the resurrection and ascension of our LORD and SAVIOR JESUS CHRIST is very important to portray because if not, it is a good chance that you are way off course. "**Then they that gladly received His word were baptized and the same day there was added unto them about three thousand souls.**" Acts 2:41

The Bible states, "**And they [*the early church*] continued steadfastly in the apostles' doctrine and fellowship, and in breaking of bread, and in prayers.**" Acts 2:42

The first observation here is the early Christians continued steadfastly or without wavering in the apostles' doctrine. Therefore, "What exactly is the apostles' doctrine ?" needs to be addressed. The Bible, the WORD of GOD, has to provide the answer. The apostle's doctrine was absolutely no different than that which was preached and proclaimed by all the holy prophets up to and including John the Baptist, and there should be a continuum of the same doctrine with the churches of today. For JESUS Himself proclaimed, **"Search the scriptures; for in them ye think ye have eternal life; and they are they which testify of me."** Jn. 5:39 The only scriptures they had and used at that time were the Old Testament scriptures. The apostles taught to love the Lord with all your heart and to love each other as yourself. To put God first in your life as mentioned in Deuteronomy. **"And thou shalt love the Lord thy God with all thine heart, and with all thy soul, and with all they might."** Deut. 6:5 Second, to love your neighbor as yourself was taught by the early apostles of Christ. **"Thou shalt not avenge, nor bear any grudge against the children of thy people, but thou shalt love thy neighbor as thyself."** Lev. 19:18 Notice when Jesus explained to the lawyer that was tempting Him, **"Thou shalt love the Lord thy God with all thy heart, and with all thy soul, and with all thy mind. And the second is like unto it, Thou shalt love thy neighbor as thyself."** Matt. 37 and 39 He was simply quoting from the Old Testament.

Another aspect the early church displayed that is uniquely different from most churches of today is how they shared not only food and clothing but also their resources and property until every man had all things in common. If considered with intellectual thought, what other way could it have been? There could not have been some big I's and little U's where some Christians were living large and others were meagerly scraping by and call themselves satisfying the commandment by Jesus, "of loving thy neighbor as thyself."

With the focus on love for God and one's fellow man hung all the laws and prophets. Jesus Himself sums it all up in the New Testament when He said, **"Thou shall love the Lord thy God with all thine heart and with all thy soul, and with all thy mind, and with all thy strength; this is the first** commandment. And the second is like it, namely this; Thou shalt love thy neighbor as thyself. There is none other commandment greater than these." Mk 12:30 and 31

This is known to be the doctrine the early disciples adhered to and lived by. If they had not, they would not have received the power from on high as Jesus promised. These simple doctrines are the same ones that should be applied and lived by in this day and age as well. There should be no difference! There should not be a Christian coming to church in their brand-new shining Jaguar with two more parked in the four-car garage at home while another humble Christian is walking unnoticed to and from church week to week and scourging to buy food possibly raiding garbage cans to eat. There are two contrasting lifestyles here concerning the Christian Church and the Christian lifestyle in general.

Let us consider John the Baptist, Jesus says of him, **"For I say unto you, 'Among those that are born of women there is not a greater prophet than John the Baptist: but he that is least in the kingdom of GOD is greater than he.'"** Lk 7:28 Now a man to receive that high of recognition from God himself needs further examination. I mean when you look at Moses who was called the friend of God, or Daniel who was called greatly beloved by God or at Jeremiah or Isaiah or Elijah or David or any of the strong prophets or high-ranking men of God. None of them was it said as said of John the Baptist by God Himself. So let us look a little closer at the person of John the Baptist for a moment.

For it to be mentioned by Christ that, "There is no man born of women greater than John the Baptist," then it stands to reason that John is a standard of one extreme of approbation by God. On the other hand, if John is a standard of approbation by God on one extreme, then logic holds that there must be another lifestyle extreme that is not approved by God. John's mission was to prepare the way of the Lord. He was to bring men to a place of repentance with the acknowledgment and forgiveness of their sins through the coming Messiah. He, John the Baptist, lived in simple housing. He wore simple clothing. And he ate simple foods. He did not drive a Jag to church! In other words, John the Baptist lived a simple unworldly lifestyle with a main focus of living for and serving the Lord and others without self-service or worldly flare. If we look at his unworldly lifestyle and give him the handle of John the Unworldly, this would be one extreme. Keep in mind that this is the one much approved by God simply because it is unworldly.

Now look at the other extreme. This person never acknowledges God. They put themselves before good works and God. They love the finest of the world consuming their time with seeking materialistic goods, money, and worldly flare (not necessarily that they have them but seeks them), exotic houses and cars, the finest of clothes and food, always seeking worldly amusements and entertainments. Let's call this person John the Worldly because their primary focus is worldliness. And there are those all around even in the church that meets this description. (Before you start to look around, take a look at yourself first.) **"Love not the world, neither the things that are in the world. If any man loves the world, the love of the Father is not in him."** 1 John 2:15

If placing these two extremes—John the Worldly on one end of the spectrum and John the Unworldly on the other end—and placing yourself between the two, where in your heart would you fit in? This is a precept that every soul-searching God-fearing Christian should focus on and seriously contemplate due to the fact that your salvation is directly dependent on which way your heart and your thinking gravitate toward. If your thoughts and actions are more closely related to the early church and the early apostles, then you are bent more toward John the Unworldly (John the Baptist) as opposed to the churches of today where people's teachings and thoughts are bending more toward John the Worldly.

Go ahead, pause a moment to do a personal analysis and place yourself on Bro. Lee's John Scale between 1 and 10. The number 1 represents the extremity of John the Worldly and 10 represent the other extremity of John the Unworldly. If you fall anywhere at five and below, you need quick repentance and rededication. The scale should represent your devotion to God, how you treat your fellow man, where you go, how you talk, how you dress, how vain you are, what you do in your spare time, what you look at, your entertainment, your amusements, what spans your mind most of a given day, etc. If most things you do, say, and watch on a daily basis as a professed Christian resembles or mimics most of the world, then you should honestly place yourself somewhere low on the scale because your life favors that of John the Worldly. If however your actions are opposite to those of John the Worldly and more unlike the world, then you may with all honesty place yourself somewhere on the upper end of the scale. Think about it and speak your mind. **"And be not conformed to this world: but be ye transformed by the renewing of your mind, that you may prove what is that good, and acceptable, and perfect, will of God."** Rom. 12:2

It is virtually impossible to have a lifestyle at this point.

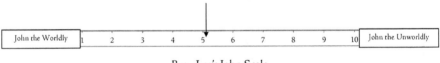

Bro. Lee's John Scale

The reason for this scenario is due to the fact that John the Baptist came in the spirit and power of Elijah to make straight a highway for our GOD. **"And His disciples asked Him, saying, 'Why then say the scribes that Elijah must first come?' And Jesus answered and said unto them, 'Elijah truly shall first come, and restore all things . . . But I say unto you, that Elijah is come already, and they knew him not, but have done unto him whatsoever they listed. Likewise shall also the Son of man suffer of them' . . . Then the disciples understood that He spake unto them of John the Baptist"** Matt. 17:10–13. Remember the prophet Elijah how his life style favored that of John the unworldly and how he never tasted death but because his life was fully devoted to serving God and his fellow man, he was carried up to heaven in chariots of fire.

The John Scale is only a visual representation of where a person may view themselves relative to worldliness or Godliness. For a person to actually be positioned at value 5 on the scale is not a reality because that would hold the same premise as one cannot straddle the fence or walk the center line of good and evil. In other words, your lifestyle is either favoring that of John the Worldly or John the Unworldly; it cannot be both.

Jesus taught the twelve apostles for roughly three and a half years the true meaning of Christianity, and if you pay close attention, His primary objective was to teach men not to be too concerned about this world. **"And the cares of this world, and the deceitfulness of riches, and the lusts of other things entering in, choke the Word, and it becometh unfruitful."** Mk 4:19 And after the LORD's resurrection, the apostles continued on this same course preaching and teaching self-denial and repentance unto salvation in the name of our LORD JESUS CHRIST. John baptized unto repentance on Him that was to come, and the apostles baptized unto Him who had come. Both baptized unto our LORD and SAVIOR JESUS CHRIST. The former was before CHRIST began His earthly ministry, and the latter was after He had come and ascended on high. **"Then Peter said unto them, 'Repent, and be baptized every one of you in the name of JESUS CHRIST for the remission of sins, and ye shall receive the gift of the HOLY GHOST.'"** Acts 2:38

Okay. The first thing for all who have ever sinned (that means all of us) to do is to continue in the apostles' doctrine. That is to come to the Messiah and *repent*. It must be understood that there can be no true repentance without knowledge of a crucified SAVIOR. So what is repentance? Merriam-Webster defines repent as (1) to turn from sin and resolve to reform one's life, (2) to feel sorry for (something done), and (3) regret. The word repent is a verb which is an action word. There must first be recognition that your life is out of harmony with GOD's will. That you may be going to church and even holding an office in church, or singing in the choir but living a life of sin and that you are in need of a crucified SAVIOR. Second, you are to confess and *turn* from your sins and on bent knees surrender all to JESUS who is the only one that can wash your sins away. Amen.

So often forgiveness is asked of sins, but in the heart there is not a full surrender and sins are often repeated. At times, the sin or sins continue without hesitation especially when there is a belief that no one else is watching or when the sin cannot readily be detected by others.

There is in fact someone watching, there is someone looking on, there is an all-seeing eye, there is someone who knows every detailed aspect of your life better than you, and a very accurate record is being kept! The name is the same one that we claim to be giving our sins to and of whom we so often pretend to surrender our all. And the name is JESUS. JESUS sees all! There is nothing hid from Him. No matter how late at night you go tippin', sippin', dippin', or trippin', or when you covet (hiding something in your heart) or lie, it does not matter; GOD sees you, and He sees it! **"For God shall bring every work into judgment, and every secret thing, whether it be good, or whether it be evil."** Ecc. 12:14 **"And I beheld, and, lo, in the midst of the throne and of the four beasts, and in the midst of the elders, stood a Lamb as it had been slain, having seven horns and seven eyes, which are the seven Spirits of God sent forth into all the earth."** Rev. 5:6

Not only should an immediate turning from sinful ways take place but repent and give them to JESUS. You should also stop trying to find self-satisfying resolve for personal problems but give them to the one who only can fix all troubles and make things right in your life if you just simply give it all to HIM. *"All to JESUS I surrender, All to HIM I freely give; I will ever love and trust HIM, In HIS presence daily live; I surrender all, I surrender all; All to THEE, my blessed SAVIOR, I surrender all."* Hymnal

Now after gaining this knowledge of a crucified SAVIOR and coming to a full repentance, not half, not three-fourths, but a full turnaround and a complete surrender to JESUS; it is time to be baptized. No lifesaving payments have to be made; no long journeys or pilgrimages are ordered. You don't have to beat yourself and go into isolation. There is no need of anything for the repentant to give or to offer except his heart. *"Nothing in my hands I bring, simply to Thy cross I cling."* A fully surrendered heart is acceptable to Jesus.

Now let's take a look at the act of baptism. The word baptize is defined as to submerge or to dip and go under water. The act of baptism is a public expression of spiritual rebirth or exemplifies the death, burial, and resurrection of Jesus. **"Know ye not, that so many of us as were baptized into Jesus Christ were baptized into His death?"** Rom. 6:3 The act of baptism itself does not cleanse the sins of the individual, neither does the water. There is no magic in the water, and all the bleach added won't help! In other words, you can go down dry coveting iniquity in your heart and come up wet harboring corruption. The sinner must believe by faith that he is dying to self and coming up living a new life in CHRIST JESUS. Thus, as CHRIST went down and was buried in the tomb and was resurrected, the repentant sinner exemplifies this as he goes down into the watery grave burying old ways and self to come up a new creature in CHRIST. **"And now why tarriest thou? Arise, and be baptized, and wash away thy sins, calling on the name of the Lord."** Acts 22:16 Burying John the Worldly and coming up a new creature in CHRIST JESUS! Would you say amen? Christ Himself is our example baptized of John the Unworldly. **"Then cometh Jesus from Galilee to Jordon unto John, to be baptized of him."** Matt. 3:13

If everything up to this point is done with sincerity of heart, then the HOLY SPIRIT will begin to do a work in you. This is that clean recognizable and unconfused receiving of the Holy Spirit. **"Then Peter said unto them, 'Repent, and be baptized every one of you in the name of Jesus Christ for the remission of sins, and ye shall receive the gift of the Holy Ghost."**

Acts 2:38 In other words, your spiritual gifts will become manifested, and as you exercise your talents, they will become stronger and stronger. You will develop more peace. Love for your fellow man will increase. Your tolerance to get irritated and your patience levels will rise. Simply stated, you become a better person to live and to get along with. You would even like yourself more when you give your life to CHRIST. It is HIM by way of the HOLY GHOST in you that makes it all good. **"To whom God would make known what is the riches of the glory of this mystery among the gentiles, which is Christ in you, the hope of Glory . . . Whom we preach, warning every man, and teaching every man in all wisdom; that we may present every man <u>perfect</u> in Christ Jesus."** Col. 1:27 and 28 **"Therefore if any man be in Christ, he is a new creature: old things are passed away; behold, all things are become new."** 2 Cor. 5:17

Now as the new Christian or convert continue in growth, they should not waver but walk steadfastly in the truth. To be like a tree planted by the rivers of water with the roots down deep; I shall not be moved. **"That we henceforth be no more children, tossed to and fro, carried about with every wind of doctrine, by the sleight of men, and cunning craftiness, whereby they lie in wait to deceive; But speaking the truth in love, may grow up into Him in all things, which is the head, even CHRIST."** Eph. 4:14 and 15

When following true Christian principles (the apostle's doctrine) and growing therein, there is an automatic tendency to traverse to the next phase of the HOLY walk that is mentioned in Acts 2:42 and is consistent with "true fellowshipping."

According to Merriam-Webster again, definition of the word fellowship or the act of "fellowshipping" is fellowship (1) the condition of *friendly* relationship existing among persons: *comradeship*, (2) a community of interest or feeling, (3) a group with similar interest. The word friendly is an interesting word in the first definition. How many church members are at odds with each other and claim to be Christians? There are individual and family feuds

130

right within the church. There are in some churches more finger-pointing and criticizing than at a televised United States presidential debate!

In order to have spiritual godliness and spiritual growth, GOD's church needs for all of its members to be on one accord. So was it with the early church. **"And they, [the church] continuing daily with one accord in the temple [the church building], and breaking bread from house to house, did eat their meat with gladness, and singleness of heart. Praising <u>GOD</u> and having favor with all the people. And the LORD <u>added</u> to the church daily such as should be saved."** Acts 2:46 and 47 The bickering, backbiting, and hatred need to cease in order for church growth to take place. GOD will not operate within an unholy environment, and He certainly will not bless mess. And by the way, just because a church may have a large congregation does not necessarily mean that it is blessed by GOD. It can be prosperous but by some power other than GOD **(the prosperity of the wicked)**. As a matter of fact, some of these vast congregations may need to check themselves to be certain that they are indeed of GOD or some other wealth-giving power. **"To the law and to the testimony: if they speak not according to this WORD, it is because there is no light in them."** Isa. 8:20 Certain churches may have powerful and eloquent speakers, good entertainment and antics, excellent drama and showmanship programs/activities, beautiful singing and music, comedy and jokes, and very dynamic family life centers. Many worldly enterprises and activities can abide within the church. But it does not mean that it came from Almighty GOD! And if it is not of GOD, there is but one and only one other entity it could have originated from, and that is the devil, the arch deceiver. He tempted Jesus with one of the same rewards that some of these mega churches seem to be receiving from him. And that is much power and glory if they would but fall down and worship him. **"Again, the devil taketh Him up into an exceeding high mountain, and sheweth Him all the kingdoms of the world, and the glory of them; And saith unto Him, 'All these things will I give Thee, if Thou wilt fall down** and worship me.' Then saith Jesus unto him, 'Get thee hence, satan: for it is written, thou shalt worship the Lord thy God, and Him only shalt thou serve." Matt. 4:8–10

Remember that Satan and his ministers can pose as an angel of light. So well will be his deceptions that he could almost fool the very elect. **"For such are false apostles, deceitful workers, transforming themselves into the apostles of CHRIST. And no marvel; for Satan himself is transformed into an angel of light. Therefore it is no great thing if his <u>ministers</u> also be transformed as the ministers of righteousness; whose end shall be according to their works."** 2 Cor. 11:13–15 There are people standing in pulpits posing as ministers of light when in fact they are ministers of darkness and deceit.

Please realize the fact that the devil, the enemy of all righteousness, is not going to approach you with some monstrous pitchfork-welding demonic look, as something that might be seen in a horror movie. People would not come to church if he did that. Also, he would not attempt to procure your homage speaking things that would not make you feel good either. He would speak smooth things while practicing lies and deceits. **"For the time will come when they will not endure sound doctrine; but after their own lusts shall they heap to themselves teachers, having itching ears; And they shall turn away their ears from the truth, and shall be turn unto fables."** 2 Tim. 4:3 and 4

In other words, according to the gospel from Paul to Timothy, there will come a time when church folk do not want to hear the truth. I submit to you reader, that that time has long since come and has almost become the so-called Christian standard! It now appears that many would rather hear smooth sugarcoated lies than the truth! And this text is not talking about people on the streets or unbelieving non-churchgoing folks. It is referring to those who rise up and go to church every week and even more so may hold offices in the church! Also, there are those who need to take into account, and the WORD of GOD makes it clear that false teachers will occupy the pulpit in the name of CHRIST. **"For there shall arise false Christs, and** false prophets [*false preachers and teachers*], and shall show great signs and wonders; insomuch that, if it were possible, they shall deceive the very elect." Matt. 24:24

The utmost care should be taken to not be deceived by so-called good-looking (or not so good-looking), smooth-talking, popular preachers who are not preaching a straight "Thus saith the Lord! Male or female, black or white, young or old, remember Satan comes in all shapes, colors, and sizes. **"For there shall arise false Christs, and false prophets, and shall shew great signs and wonders; insomuch that, if it were possible, they shall deceive the very elect."** Matt. 24:24

Do not be so naive to think for one moment that everyone who stands in a pulpit is of GOD! And do not be so naive to think that the pastor who stands before you from week to week is exempt from this text of the Bible. This is the very reason why the apostle Paul explained to Timothy, **"Study to show thyself approved unto GOD, a workman that needeth not to be ashamed, rightly dividing the WORD of truth."** 2 Tim. 2:15

THE EARLY CHURCH'S ORGANIZATIONAL STRUCTURE

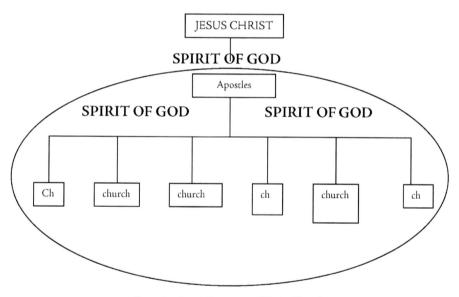

Organizational Structure of Early Church

The early church's system of organization was much different back then than it is today. Referring to the book of Acts and the above diagram, we see that CHRIST was unquestionably the head. Jesus ministers to His church by way of His Holy Spirit, which descends from above down into the church as He sees fit. All the spiritual gifts given by the Holy Spirit are for the edification of the church. After Jesus ascended on high, He was still the head of His church, but He assigned earthly leadership to His apostles, who were to lead in the spreading of HIS gospel by way of the HOLY SPIRIT's guidance. **"But the Comforter, which is the Holy Ghost, whom the Father will send in My name, He shall teach you all things, to your remembrance, whatsoever I have said unto you."** John 14:26

GOD THE FATHER, GOD THE SON, and GOD THE HOLY SPIRIT are working together today as they were back then for the saving of souls.

GOD THE FATHER

GOD THE SON

GOD THE HOLY SPIRIT

It was in this fashion the apostles were to head up the raising of the general church of which thousands were baptized not long after the outpouring of the HOLY SPIRIT. **"Then they that gladly received His word were baptized: and the same day there were added unto them about three thousand souls."** Acts 2:41

After which, it was more or less Paul's directive to begin to spread the gospel to the Gentiles in other localities. Thus individual church congregations in various localities, though some may have been smaller than the main church in Israel, but they still were very much integral parts of the systematic whole. That is all churches at this time were part of the whole body in one faith under God. Keep in mind, they were still of **"One LORD, one faith, and one baptism."** Eph. 4:5 even though they were spread out. There were not thousands of different denominations of different beliefs. There was then and always has been One Lord, one faith, and one baptism of the Christian Church! That's it! Keep in mind that the true Christian Church arose out of Judaism. No other aspect of the church existed immediately following the resurrection of Christ. Only the Jews and Gentiles that followed Christ's teachings were members of His church. Judaism continued on its wayward course along with all other nonbelieving idol-worshipping pagan religions in the world at that time. After Christ's ascension into heaven there were many religions but there was one and only one Christian denomination at that time, and the same should be at this present day.

Some of the churches established by Paul and other disciples at that time were larger than others, but they each had equal access to GOD by way of the HOLY SPIRIT, and they were all on one accord and of one faith. As indicated by the diagram of the early church's organizational structure above. The varying sizes of the rectangles and squares denote how some churches may have been larger or smaller than another. No one church superseded the other based on quantitative numerical size, and their order of service was pretty much the same. Each church, as long as it was holistically following

Christ, received spiritual guidance by God regardless of size. Also because they were all on one accord and had unity in the faith, (one Lord, one faith, and one baptism) it did not matter whether you worshipped in Antioch or Capernaum; the preaching and worship services were for the most part similar even as it was in the Old Testament times. If congregations got off track, no matter how large or how far away, Paul or some other disciple of Christ would often go back to correct them. It was very important to the early workers of the gospel that they stayed true to the universal principle of "one Lord, one faith, and one baptism." **"All scripture is given by inspiration of God, and is profitable for doctrine, for reproof, for correction, for instruction in righteousness."** 2 Tim. 3:16

After the people came to CHRIST and learned of Him, they humbled themselves and practiced Christianity in its truest and purest form. They learned of Him not just know of His name and do whatever they want. Christianity was in its infancy. Early Christians were not trying to be exalted in any fashion or outdo anybody else, nor did they seek to draw attention to themselves. They did not indicate in any way that their congregation was better than others. They did not set up partitions, real or unreal, of various church groups or bodies. They did not say things like, "I like my church better than theirs." or "Our church has more people, so it must be more blessed." Well, you must note that GOD can accomplish His will with few in number as with a great multitude. Numbers are not a prerequisite with GOD. Often men of God would be told to reduce the numbers because they had too many, as in the case of Gideon. To tell the truth of the matter, He said, **"Strive to enter in at the strait gate: for *many*, I say unto you, will seek to enter in, and shall not be able."** Lk 13:24 If many seek to enter and not be able, then the contrast to that would be that only a few will indeed enter in at the straight gate while many fall short.

Also, the church at that time did not exalt themselves. As a matter of fact, the early church understood better than most what JESUS meant when they were trying to determine which of them should be the greatest in the kingdom to come. JESUS said unto them, **"If any man desires to be first, the same shall be last of all, and servant of all."** Mk 9:35 Again, He said to them, **"For he that is least among you all, the same shall be great."** Lk 9:48 JESUS made this statement not only to the apostles but to any man who seeks to be first with Him. They were never to exalt themselves, but by the power of GOD, they were to with humility proclaim the gospel to all men. **"Humble yourselves in the sight of the Lord, and He shall lift you up."** James 4:10

To that end, they would be exalted at the day of CHRIST's return. Only then would they receive their just reward. This was not for clergy only but to any person wanting a closer walk with the LORD. If any prerequisite is needed, humility is the order of the day. **"He hath showed thee, O man, what is good; and what doth the LORD require of thee, but to do justly and to love mercy, and to walk <u>humbly</u> with thy GOD."** Mic 6:8

From the pulpit to the farthest pew in the church building, there is a need for a serious revival in humility. Returning unto the old ways and the straight paths is something God would be pleased in seeing His off-course children doing. "Thus saith the LORD, **'Stand ye in the ways, and see, and ask for the old paths, where is the good way, and walk therein, and ye shall find rest for your souls.' But they said, 'We will not walk therein.'"** Jer. 6:16

CHRIST JESUS is the head, the apostles were the leaders of GOD's newly developing church and this need to be made crystal clear, every follower of CHRIST, is today as it was then, a disciple of CHRIST regardless of the position or rank held. In other words, an apostle was a disciple, an evangelist was a disciple, a deacon was a disciple, and the church's clerk was one if they did GOD's will. Any church member who followed CHRIST was a *disciple* of His. It did not matter what church office they held as long as they were a true follower of JESUS. Amen. From the least to the greatest, JESUS only sees and knows the heart of the individual that is striving to follow Him to the fullest capacity that their frail human hearts will allow, not office, position, nor rank. The only difference is that the higher the position, the greater the responsibility. **"For unto whomsoever much is given, of him shall be much required."** Lk 12:48

A good example of this is Stephen. Stephen was a deacon in the early church, but he was a disciple as were all members of the church who were seeking only to do GOD's will.

If you are a student of prophecy, then you know that according to the book of Daniel it was by the stoning of Stephen, the probationary period had ended for the Jews. Using the biblical standard of one day equals one year principle when considering prophetic periods. "After the number of the days, in which ye searched the land, even forty days, each day for a year, shall ye bear your iniquities, even forty years, and ye shall know My breach of promise." Num. 14:34 Also see Ezekiel 4:6 also in support of this day for a year principle in Bible prophecy. The prophetic seventy years or four hundred and ninety literal years that was to be determined upon the Jewish people mentioned by Daniel the prophet, ended with the martyrdom of Stephen. (These prophetic texts can be found in the book of Daniel. However, it is not the scope of this book to go into the deep prophetic messages of the books of Daniel and Revelation. Nevertheless, it is encouraged that the reader and the ardent students of scripture with much prayer turn to GOD for a deeper understanding of these great books of the Bible.)

Stephen was just a simple deacon. Not an apostle, prophet, evangelist, nor even the least of these—a preacher or teacher—but just a humble deacon that GOD selected to use for His purposes to fulfill prophecy. The Jewish people were the chosen to deliver the gospel message to the entire world, but when they rejected the calling and sealed their fate by the killing of Stephen (one of CHRIST's disciples), the gospel was to go to the Gentiles. **"And Stephen full of faith and power did great wonders and miracles among the people."** Acts 6:8 therefore all that followed CHRIST were disciples of CHRIST. The HOLY SPIRIT did GOD's bidding by establishing certain positions of the church for the edifying and for operation of the church. Church organization was for the sole purpose of the spreading of the gospel's end time message and to turn the hearts of men to CHRIST in an organized manner. It was not for the purposes of week to week entertainment. There were given various gifts of the SPIRIT to all the disciples (the followers of GOD) to accomplish this worldwide endeavor. **"Now there are diversities of gifts, but the same SPIRIT. And there are differences of administrations, but the same LORD. And there are diversities of operations, but it is the same GOD which worketh all in all. But the manifestation of the SPIRIT is given to every man to prophet withal. For to one is given by the SPIRT, the WORD of wisdom, to another the WORD of knowledge by the same SPIRIT; To another faith by the same SPIRIT; to another gifts of healing by the same SPIRIT; To another the working of miracles; to another prophecy; to another discerning of spirits; to another divers kinds of tongues** [*the ability to speak in other languages without schooling*]**; to another the interpretation of tongues** [*the ability to understand a foreign language*]**: But all these worketh that one and selfsame SPIRIT, dividing to every man severally as He will. For as the body is one, and hath many members, and all the members of that one body, being many, is one body: so also is CHRIST."** 1 Cor. 12:4–12

Within all of these early churches that comprised one body of believers, the early Christians did not have clicks. In other words, there were not subgroups that would isolate themselves against other believers within the church. If these fragments have surfaced in your congregation, they need to be broken up before the power of God will be manifested. There were those, however, who had special friendships and hung out more with some more so than with others. But the point is, if you were a Christian back then, you were never excluded from an invitation or blackballed simply because you looked differently or because you may have had a different outlook on some particular other than Christian principle. In other words, true Christians may differ in their personal likes and dislikes, but they would always be in agreement on Christian principle and doctrine. For example, one sister may like a yellow dress as opposed to another sister who may like the blue, but they both should agree on the Christian principles of wearing the dress in a godly manner and "loving their neighbor as themselves."

Most of the early Christians, did for the most part, believe and stood fast on the one belief system. There were not five hundred different points of view on Christian faith. All were on one accord and of one faith! Today, there are hundreds of different denominations and even more different theological positions in this country alone, not to mention other countries, and this just simply cannot be of GOD. GOD does not and will not generate confusion! **"I therefore, the prisoner of the LORD, beseech you that ye walk worthy of the vocation wherewith ye are called, with all lowliness and meekness, with longsuffering, forbearing one another <u>in love</u>; Endeavoring to keep <u>the unity of the SPIRIT</u> in the <u>bond of peace</u>. There is <u>one body</u>, and <u>one SPIRIT</u>, even as ye are called in <u>one hope</u> of your calling; <u>One LORD</u>, <u>one faith</u>, and <u>one</u> baptisim, <u>One GOD</u>, and FATHER of all, who is above all, and through all, and in you all."** Eph. 4:1–6

These texts are really self-explanatory. There was one body or in other words one church, one denomination. We all know that there is one and only one GOD. **"Ye are My witnesses, saith the LORD, and My servant whom I have chosen: that ye may know and believe Me, and understand that I am He: Before Me there was no god formed, neither shall there be after Me."** Isa. 43:10

There is only one SPIRIT the Comforter. **"But <u>the COMFORTER, which is the HOLY SPIRIT</u>, whom the FATHER will send in My name, He shall teach you all things, and bring all things to your remembrance, whatsoever I have said unto you."** Jn. 14:26

The question begs itself: How in the world did all of this spiritual confusion creep or seep into the test tube? And the question can only be answered and explained by the Word of God. The Bible clearly shows that it could have come from one and only one source. Not of GOD because He is not the author of confusion. **"For GOD is not the author of confusion,** but <u>of peace</u> as in <u>all</u> churches of the saints." 1 Cor. 14:33 Be clear that when this text mentions "all churches of the saints," it is not talking about many different denominations but of the one body of Christ that are in different localities.

It does not say, but of peace in some churches, but it says, "but of peace in *all* churches of the saints." Paul here is referring to all the churches of one faith because after the resurrection of Jesus, there was only "one Lord, one faith, and one baptism." Again, he is speaking about all the churches of one faith in many different localities. Do not be misled to think that he is referring to several different denominations when he says, "All churches." He is not! However, if there is no peace in your church, no matter which one you belong to, then some power other than GOD is reigning over it! The enemy of souls is the author of confusion, and it is by him that all these different denominations and theological positions exist in the first place. (Bear in mind the needle in the haystack analogy that will be reviewed shortly.) Every last person on this planet who is attempting to serve the true GOD with a whole heart needs fervent prayer and a diligent searching of scripture to get on and to stay on the right course. Amen. **"Study to show thyself approved unto GOD, a workman that needeth not to be ashamed, rightly dividing the word of truth."** 2 Tim. 2:15

Again JESUS's advice to us is **"Search the scriptures: for in them ye think ye have eternal life: and they are they that testify of Me."** Jn. 5:39 Study for yourself and ask of GOD who imparts wisdom, knowledge, and understanding to whomsoever should ask of Him. **"If any of you lack wisdom, let him ask of GOD, that giveth to all men liberally, and upbraideth not; and it shall be given him."** James 1:5 that the man of GOD may be perfect thoroughly furnished unto all good works.

There will be absolutely no excuse for not seeking out and finding the absolute truth as GOD would have you to know it for yourself. You will indeed be held accountable for every sermon you have heard and every book you should have read to seek out a deeper understanding of our LORD and our CREATOR. **"But seek ye first the kingdom of God, and His righteousness, and all these things shall be added unto you."** Matt. 6:33

Another thing to take note of concerning the early church with respect to the fellowshipping aspect under observation is the fact that one Christian respected another. Certainly there were probably some disagreements on personal matters and even then "turning the other cheek" was often employed, but when it came to the Word of GOD, all disciples of Christ agreed. Otherwise, the Bible would be a lie, because it reiterates with resounding clarity, "that they were all on one accord." Don't you wish this could be said of your church? They followed the principles that every Christian in every age should follow and that is what CHRIST Himself instituted. How on earth did today's professed Christians get ever so far off course with the ideology of Christianity is in itself somewhat of a mystery? And it should not come as a surprise to anyone seeking the straight path, for Paul wrote while he was walking the earth and preaching the gospel that **"For the mystery of iniquity doth already work."** 2 Thess. 2:7

If the devil was already working in and against the church at a time when it was in its purest state, then one can only imagine, if they cannot see with a spiritual eye, what has happened to the church some two thousand years down the road. A flash flood is readily seen, but a slow rising one is hardly noticeable. So it is with changes that man makes within the church. One by one, worldly changes creep in and over time, they are not readily noticeable. Church operations, worship, and interactions appear as if things have always operated this way, and there is no real feeling of a need for change. Periodically, churches over time need to check themselves because they may be teaching for doctrine the commandments of men. And there is definitely a need to be on guard against such changes. Surely, they may give a good show, but are they truly following the practices of GOD, or are they teaching for doctrines the commandments of men? This is just one of the questions that every professed Christian should ask themselves based on the only true reference—the Bible. And it is very important to remember that there has always only been one true church. There may be sheep in other churches, but there is only one true church! At the time when the nation of Israel was set up as GOD's church, there were other theological beliefs and other religions being practiced all around them but only one true church. When CHRIST came, He continued in the church that had been set up since the fall of man. The recognizable church (the then-known temple) was in apostasy along with the other religious practices of the day. As a point of note, some of the other religious practices of the day had crept into the true church. They had idols sitting in the temple of God. Can you imagine that? If they were setting up idols in God's church back then, you can only imagine what is being set up in God's church today. They had also rejected the Messiah. Jesus could hardly preach and teach in His own church buildings! He often had to assemble down by the riverside or at the Mount of Olives or somewhere. Remember there are many churches but only one church! And if there are idols in God's true church, just imagine what's going on in the other churches so called. JESUS was explaining to some of His disciples that there were other sheep that were not of this fold (the true church), but that He Himself would bring them into His fold the only true church that has ever been. **"And other sheep I have, which are not of this fold: them also I must bring, and they shall hear My voice; and there shall be one fold, and one Shepherd."** Jn. 10:16

Often people make the mistake believing this text is talking about when JESUS returns, there will be one church with many people from many different denominations and many different theological belief systems. This is not the case. JESUS is coming back for the true church that is here now and that has always been here. There are, however, people of GOD who have not heard the whole truth that are still unknowingly practicing falsehoods under the banner of Christianity. They just simply don't know. God will send somebody or something their way to lead them to the truth, and when they hear the truth (if they are diligently seeking for the truth, the truth will definitely come their way), they will respond and come to the light. At that time, Jesus would make them now part of the fold. Because the LORD said, "Them also I must bring, and they shall hear MY voice; and there shall be one fold, and one Shepherd." I repeat: there has always been one true religious practice, one true church, one LORD, one truth. When JESUS returns the second time, He is coming back for that church, the group of people who love the LORD their GOD with all of their heart and who love their neighbors as themselves. They are respecting one another and helping one another at all times. Not only when an emergency occurs, as in the case of the 9/11 attacks when everyone came together to help. Not only in a spirit of giving at Christmas time but at all times. All Christian experiences should be just that—Christ like.

When a true follower of CHRIST, no matter where they are or which religious system they are practicing or following, when they hear His voice, they will pursue a straight thus saith the LORD! They will become a part of the true fold of GOD that has existed since the beginning of time because they listened to the voice of GOD and are moved by the impress of the HOLY SPIRIT! They will not harden their hearts and say things like, "I already have my church and my pastor." Or they hear the voice of GOD and see where the WORD of GOD makes all the sense in the world, but they will respond by saying things like, "Let me go ask my pastor to see if this is what GOD is saying!" The WORD speaketh expressly, and they need to check with man! For the WORD of GOD clearly says, **"Come out of her, My people, that ye be not partakers of her sins, and that ye receive not of her plagues."** Rev. 18:4 This is referring to the coming out of false doctrines and false religions.

After CHRIST was crucified pretty much by what was the populace's view of the church, the true church continued on. A lot of its members were in hiding for fear of meeting the same fate as their Lord, but it still existed. During the time of the preaching and writing of Paul, there was only one true church. Even down through the Dark Ages, you had the true church (of which millions of true Christians gave their lives), and there were also an apostate or false Christian Church and hundreds of other apostate beliefs, religions, idol worshipping, false gods, and theological positions that were not in harmony with GOD's WORD. There was, however, a true church in the midst of all the prevailing corruption that was pressing on, those who sought to do only GOD's will and who loved and respected their neighbors. Even though it may have been contrary to popular belief, they continued on in the faith, and many of them were martyred and slain for the truth's sake. And guess what? Christians today should also suffer persecution for the truth's sake, not to be looking for persecution, but if you are trying to lead a Godly life, it will find you. **"Yea, and all that will live Godly in CHRIST JESUS shall suffer persecution."** 2 Tim. 3:12

If you are not suffering some form of Christian persecution, then there is a good chance to believe that the devil does not see you as a threat to his dominion, not insinuating a person provoking people and bringing hardship upon themselves but rather someone who is living a God-fearing life and tries to proclaim the truth but is rejected for the truth's sake. Ultimately, you (the true Christian) will be rejected by the enemies of righteousness because JESUS CHRIST lives in you. **"If the world hates you, ye know that it hated me before it hated you. If ye were of the world, the world would love his own: but because ye are not of the world, but I have chosen you out of the world, therefore the world hateth you."** Jn. 15:18 and 19

All through the ages every person had an opportunity to come to the truth. Even though they were practicing falsehoods, they had a chance to hear the truth. In Noah's day, he preached for a hundred and twenty years, and only his family came to the truth. Do not be caught up in the belief that because you are a member of a large congregation or of a large following, that you have the truth or the right belief system. That is one of the biggest fallacies in Christendom. People believing that simply because of large numbers, they must have the truth and are in the right place usually are making a large mistake! Again, Jesus says seek to enter in at the straight gate, "**Enter ye in at the strait gate, for wide is the gate, and broad is the way, that leadeth to destruction, and <u>many</u> there be which go in thereat: Because strait is the gate, and narrow is the way, which leadeth unto life, and <u>few</u> there be that find it.**" Matt. 7:13 and 14

In Noah's day, the larger denominations were wrong and destroyed. They laughed and jeered at him, but it was they who were going the wrong way. Remember the old adage, "They that laugh last laughs best." Jesus says to the faithful, "**Blessed are ye that hunger now; for ye shall be filled. Blessed are ye that weep now: for ye shall laugh. Blessed are ye, when men shall hate you, and when they shall separate you from their company, and shall reproach you, and cast out your name as evil, for the son of man's sake. Rejoice in that day, and leap for joy: for, behold, your reward is great in heaven: for in the like manner did their fathers unto the prophets.**" Lk 6:21-23

In Noah's and Israel's day, the larger denominations were wrong. In CHRIST's day when He walked the earth, the larger denominations were wrong. In Martin Luther's day, the larger denominations were wrong, and so it has been in every age thereafter. With lots of prayer, seek out the truth with prayer and look it up for yourself. Do not be deceived by numbers nor by activities or fundamental practices but come to the knowledge of GOD by much prayer and studying of His WORD.

What a person sees when they join or encounter a particular church is what they perceive the church to be whether it is following GODLY principles or not. They really do not know. It is what everybody else is doing, so it must be okay. Following the crowd seems to be the practice of the day. "It makes me feel good," some say. Or because some churches stir up a lot of noise and excitement, you might hear something like, "They've got it goin' on over there at that church, sister girl." Your eternal salvation is at stake if you follow this line of reasoning, theological deduction, or seduction. Instead of going to your LORD and SAVIOR JESUS CHRIST pleading for knowledge and wisdom, they look around and follow the crowd or look to see what feels good!

Certainly, make no mistake, when an individual receives the impress of the HOLY SPIRIT and the indwelling of JESUS CHRIST in the heart, they will feel great! Burdens will be lifted, chains of guilt will be broken, and there will be joy in the heart. But this is not to be confused with false excitement of emotionalisms or sensationalisms. Some people may feel good after leaving a nightclub or a secular concert or after they have taken a drink or after taking a hit or two of cocaine. There may be a feeling of blitz and ecstasy just because it feels good, but it's not the clean kind that is associated by having an exhilarating portion of the HOLY GHOST! Actually, your Christian walk should have absolutely nothing to do with feelings. **"Now the just shall live by faith: but if any man draws back, My soul shall have no pleasure in him."** Heb. 10:38 **"So likewise ye, when ye shall have done all those things which are commanded you, say, 'We are unprofitable servants: for we have done that which was our duty to do.'"** Lk 17:10

You may not be in a good mood or even feel like praying on any given day, but it is still your unquestionable duty to serve the Almighty GOD, whether you feel like it or not! That is, if you are a child of GOD and not simply following the crowd nor just going along with the flow. This is one of the biggest mistakes within the Christian walk of faith. People should always love one another, help one another, and show genuine concern for one another as long as they are in agreement concerning Christian principles, then they are truly Christian. If two Christian friends strive together and one along the way decides to yoke up and follow the world as opposed to following GOD, then this is where the two friends should separate and part company. This should become the proverbial "fork in the road." **"Be ye not unequally yoked with** unbelievers: for what fellowship hath righteousness with unrighteousness? And what communion hath light with darkness?" 2 Cor. 6:14

You just simply cannot be friends with the world and friends with GOD. "Ye adulterers and adulteresses, know ye not that the friendship of the world is enmity with GOD? Whosoever therefore will be a friend of the world is the enemy of GOD." Jas 4:4

You cannot walk with the world or with false or apostate religions and claim to be a friend of, let alone, a child of GOD. "They are not of the world, even as I am not of the world." Jn. 17:16

There should be every attempt by Christians to win the individual that walk in darkness over to CHRIST's marvelous light. To love and be friendly with all is also a requirement. But to strive with them, to converse with them in un-Christian talk and to walk with them in places Christians should not walk, to link up with them in darkness is not an admonition of the LORD. "But shun profane and vain babblings; for they will increase unto more ungodliness." 2 Tim. 2:16

Early church folk showed friendship by helping one another. "Bear ye one another's burdens, and so fulfill the law of CHRIST." Gal. 6:2 This was also indicated by the free heartedness of the early Christians one toward the other. Unlike churchy folk of today, the early Christians did not hoard everything that they owned to self. In today's capitalistic society, people are brought up from their youth to believe that they are number one and that they should get, get, get, and after you have gotten all that you can get, get some more. And not only get it but store it up and die with it in the bank! Self-preservation is the order of the day! Children are primarily raised up to have a selfish heart. I am sorry, folks, but this is not GOD's plan. JESUS said, "Take heed, and beware of covetousness: for a man's life consisteth not in the abundance of the things which he possesseth. And He spake a parable unto them, saying, 'The ground of a certain rich man brought forth plentifully.' And he said, 'This will I do: I will pull down my barns, and build greater; and there will I bestow all my fruits and my goods.' And I will say to my soul, 'Soul, thou hast much goods laid up for many years; take thine ease, eat, drink, and be merry.' But GOD said unto him, 'Thou fool, this night thy soul shall be required of thee: then whose shall those things be, which thou hast provided?' So is he that layeth up treasure for himself, and is not rich toward GOD." Lk 12:16–21

What if CHRIST behaved as selfishly as most today and had said, "Let those no good sinners die for themselves. I am going to preserve my own life down here." Then all would of a certainty be hopelessly lost. Surely GOD can and does bless individuals with wealth, but He wants them to use it to His name's honor and glory while furthering the gospel.

One biblical indication of this principle is where it was depicted in the book of Acts that the early church members would sell personal possessions and help others so that all concerned were equal and that the gospel message could go forward. Hardly ever do you hear a sermon concerning these essentials preached today in this present time. **"And all that believed were together, and had all things common; And sold their possessions and goods, and parted them to all *men*, as every man had need."** Acts 2:44 and 45

Actually, the text is simple enough to speak for itself, but where is this all too important aspect of the Christian Church today? And why is it hardly ever preached from the pulpits today? From the front to the back of the church, everyone is seeking personal gains. This distributional concept displayed by the early church reflects a beautiful ideological principle when you think about it. There was total unselfishness. The same unselfish attitude GOD had when he created the earth for man, the early Christians in Acts 2 had for each other. **"These wait all upon thee; that thou mayest give them their meat in due season. That thou givest them they gather: thou openest thine hand, they are filled with good."** Ps 104:27 and 28

In preparation for the heavenly kingdom, the early Christians unselfishly sold and got rid of worldly possessions. They imparted some of their wealth to others who were a little less fortunate. There was a very high level of concern for fellow church members. They gave so that every man had all things common as they were in need. Again, there were no big I's and no little u's. There is a lot to be gleaned concerning the unselfish acts of Christians concerning the early church in Acts, and if you read the Book of Acts, it really is self-explanatory and should for the betterment influence your acts!

On the other hand, why would it be so difficult to get today's church members to operate on these basic Christian principles having a heart of freewill giving and emptying self of worldly possessions? Simply because the test tube of earth has become so corrupt with greed and selfishness, it would seem unnatural to commit such benevolent acts read about in the book of Acts. We have gotten so far from the truth that reverting back to true Christian principles seems wrong or very difficult to do. Today, especially in this country, at most, you might get shot or at least talked about and derided if you even hinted of church folk selling everything and giving to the poor so that all would have things in common. You may be labeled a communist or something worse. Though capitalism, communism, and socialism are all political ideologies having all things common with the early church is purely from a spiritual perspective and a Godly way this is in fact according to the Word of God the way the early church practiced. It is mentioned in the early church, and it is demonstrated by the basic principle of how GOD Himself opens His hands wide to give both saint and sinner sunshine and rain. **"That ye may be the children of your Father which is in heaven: for He maketh His sun to rise on the evil and on the good, and sendeth rain on the just and on the unjust."** Matt. 5:45

Have you ever really considered the things most needed for human life GOD has unselfishly blest us with an overabundance of it? And He gives them freely. There are not any costs involved! He wanted to make certain that His children would never run out of basic physiological and biological necessities, such as sunshine, air, water, and food. A lot of folk don't deserve to breathe HIS air or to drink HIS water, much less other things received undeservingly and still have their hands and lips stuck out wanting more and wondering why they don't get it! There is plenty of water to go around. Even the poor have access to it! The poor would be in trouble if they were dependent upon the rich to supply their air for breathing. Only a merciful and almighty GOD would make all of our necessities for life available at little or no cost to a world of ungrateful sinners who don't really deserve it. He gives it any way! And those who have an overabundance should give to those who lack. Most of the time, these things given by God are all to often taken for granted! Ask yourself, how often do you thank God for the air that you breathe? Or thank Him for the water that you drink? Not to mention thanking Him for the sun that shines down on us when most of the time He hear only complaints of how hot it might be. Oh LORD, have mercy on us! If these God-given basic life-sustaining necessities ever ran out or got to a point where we could not use them anymore, we are in t-r-o-u-b-l-e! The point is that GOD blessed us with these things so that all could benefit from them, the just as well as the unjust, rich or poor, but if man mess them up, it is not GOD's fault. And once man messes up these God-given essentials, then there is a cost to clean them up!

The early Christians had a desire to operate in a Godly, unselfish manner. The early brethren also had nice fellowship dinners, not only at church, but they included the personal touch by having dinners at their homes. Today, there is a lot of pot lucking at church. Everybody brings a dish or a pot, and we will just do it right here at church. There is no real intimacy. There is nothing wrong with pot lucking at church some of the time, but more times than not, we need to interact at each other's homes, be more spiritually interactive with each other, and have that personal touch. **"And they, continuing daily with one accord in the temple, <u>and breaking bread from house to house,</u> did eat their meat with gladness and singleness of heart."** Acts 2:46

This is a beautiful concept how the early Christians could leave church (the temple) and go from house to house to eat a good wholesome Sabbath meal and be well-received by fellowship Christians. Today, you might get the door slammed in your face if you are not of the right click! And even if you are, you still might! We need, my friends, to get back to the old ways- the early Christians' ways. GOD's way! **"Thus saith the LORD, 'Stand ye in the ways, and see, and ask for the old paths, where is the good way, and walk therein, and ye shall find rest for your souls.' But they said, 'We will not walk therein.'"** Jer. 6:16

Surely we live in a fast-paced modernized society, but good solid Christian principles should never be abated. As long as we are looking for the return of the LORD of our Christian beliefs, the principles should still hold fast. **"For this is the message that ye heard from the beginning, that we should <u>love one another</u>."** 1 Jn. 3:11 GOD's WORD is as solid as a rock. It is an anchor that holds fast. It never changes. Therefore, it is up to us to look for and return to the old ways because if there is any change that has come about different today than it was back then, it is most certainly man that have changed and have gone off course, not the WORD of GOD! **"For I am the Lord, I change not; therefore ye sons of Jacob are not consumed."** Mal. 3:6

Are people living this way today? Not so much by words but by action? So often GOD offers rest, peace, joy, and happiness, but we often let self get in the way and turn from the truth.

The final aspect of the early church that will be viewed or considered under our spiritual microscope is their prayer life. Prayer for those early Christians was according to the WORD of GOD—very abundant and frequent. **"And they continued steadfastly in the apostles' doctrine and fellowship, and in breaking of bread, and in <u>prayers</u>."** Acts 2:42 They would often go entire nights with prayer. Not those long drawn-out prayers to impress the people, but the coming together of sincere Christians humbly petitioning the throne room of grace. These early Christians would show deep humility to GOD by petitioning Him while kneeling. Some people and congregations of today think that they are too sophisticated or too finely dressed to kneel before Almighty GOD in prayer. "What, mess up my suit on my knees? You must be kidding?" say some. Not referring to those because of physiological limitations cannot kneel, and even they can kneel in their hearts. But the reference is to those who think they are too good to humble themselves before an Almighty GOD. Even King Solomon, in all of his glory and wisdom, is one of many that are mentioned in the Bible that went to GOD on bent knees with his hands stretched out toward heaven to ask blessings of GOD. The principle is also demonstrated in the last book of the Bible; the book of Revelation cites John as saying, **"And I John saw these things, and heard them. And when I had heard and seen, I fell down to <u>worship</u> before the feet of the angel which showed me these things. Then saith he unto me, 'See thou do it not: for I am thy fellow servant, and of thy brethren the prophets, and of them which keep the sayings of this book: <u>worship GOD</u>."** Rev. 22:8 and 9

Here, John was given a series of visions, and he was so overwhelmed by them that he fell down at the feet of the angel who showed him these things to worship him. If John, who was a man of GOD, should mistakenly fall down and worship a created being (an angel), then how much more so should he (we) willingly fall down to worship the CREATOR who is Almighty GOD? It should also be noted that when certain individuals came to be healed of CHRIST, they would often come before Him kneeling to make their request known unto Him and to worship Him also. And they were never told to see that they do it not as was in the case with John before the strong angel. This also substantiates further the fact that CHRIST is GOD and therefore is worthy of and should be worshipped. **"And there came a leper to Him, beseeching Him, and kneeling down to Him, saying unto Him, 'If Thou wilt, Thou canst make me clean.'"** Mk 1:40

Churches and individuals should fall down and worship GOD in prayer every time prayer presents itself. He deserves it. But He, being a loving GOD, will not force you. In the end, however, those who prefer not to bow now will bow down to Him then, so they might as well get used to it and get some practice now. **"For it is written, 'As I live,' saith the LORD, 'Every knee shall bow to Me, and every tongue shall confess to GOD.'"** Rom. 14:11

Respect and honor are given to certain elected officials or judges and the likes by standing when they enter a room or when a minister enters into a worship service and some think it is somewhat difficult to pay full homage to GOD by kneeling in prayer. Humbled prayer should be the key to your devotion. From a spiritual perspective, just think about how in some churches, there is hardly any prayer at all let alone going to the throne of grace on bent knees!

Also, the reason for, as well as the concept of prayer, has been taken out of prayer meeting! It is more like prayer *meatin'* rather than prayer meeting. People will come for the loaves and fishes more so than for prayer! More prayer is needed, and it is needed right away! We need it individually as well as collectively. And there is a need to do it more humbly and respectfully. There are many different excuses why people and churches do not kneel for prayer but a couple of the more popular ones are, "The floor is too hard," "Get some pillows," or "Don't want to dirty up my suit on the floor." Wear jeans! "It's too cumbersome to kneel." Stay at home!

Even in the Old Testament book of Genesis when GOD was instructing Moses on how to build the Ark of the Covenant and the mercy sit where GOD's Shekinah glory was to dwell between the cherubim; the cherubim were to kneel and reverently face where GOD's presence was to reside. This was a model or a pattern of the true. If cherubim who are mighty in GOD's scheme of created beings are kneeling in HIS presence, how much more so should we when we go before HIM in prayer. We were created a little lower than regular angels and a lot lower than mighty cherubim. GOD is not to be mocked nor trifled with! He is due the highest respect and the highest honor that the Creator of the entire universe is due and we need to start giving it to Him today. Amen.

JESUS admonishes us to pray always. **"Watch ye therefore, and pray always, that ye may be accounted worthy to escape all these things that shall come to past, and to stand before the Son of man."** LK 21:36 Here, JESUS is concerned for all His true followers and is plainly telling us to pray always because of the fiery trials that are to come upon the earth! Diligence should be sought to take JESUS at His word! A continuous attitude of prayer should be commonplace for most Christians. Hours on end are wasted away in front of televisions, at plays, at movies, ball games, card playing, comedy shows, parties, socials, civil events, at restaurants, amusement parks, and the list goes on, while some have a very difficult time spending ten minutes on bent knees in prayer to Almighty GOD! When devotional time is spent with GOD, it should start by humble knee-bent prayer.

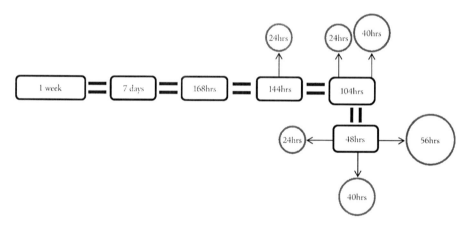

Bro. Lee's hours per week time diagram.

As the diagram shows, there are seven days in a week. There are one hundred sixty-eight hours in a seven day week period. It is the weekly hour increments we need to take a closer look at to see how our time is spent from week to week. And more specifically the remaining forty-eight hours of relative free time that God blessed us with, what are being done with those hours from week to week? Are they spent mostly on self-gratifying pleasures or is some of this time offered up to a well deserving God for His service?

Now the people who are being paid to work in the vineyard cannot consider the time spent working for which they are being compensated with the 48 hours of free time that may be offered to God for His service.

Now let's look at how our time is distributed. God gave man 168 hours of time to work with on a weekly basis. He does not force us too but He asks for a 24 hour devotion to Him on His Sabbath day. (A considerable amount of people don't even do this effectively.) If it is observed appropriately as it should be that would leave us with 144 hours per week to take care of our personal needs. Let's say that 40 hours are devoted to work for the supplying of earthly needs. This is still time that God has given to man for himself. He may work 40 hours or more or less but this is still time reserved for personal needs. After the 24 hour Sabbath is applied and 40 hours of the work week are used, there still remains 104 hours left in the week for personal maintenance and needs. Most of us do need rest so let's give the benefit of the doubt and say eight hours per day (56 hrs./wk.) are used for sleep. From the 104 hours left, 56 hours may be used for sleep consumption that would leave a grand total of 48 hours of free time to be used for additional work, dealing with children, play, amusements, entertainment, more rest, or whatever you feel a need to use it for. But the big question that poses itself for every believing Christian is how much of this 48 hour time is offered to God for His service? Actually for every Christian a large portion of this time should be devoted to the one who gave it to us in the first place and not only for self. After self-examination, if most of this free time is given over to T.V. watching, other entertainments, amusements, and other self-gratifying activities then the Christian walk needs to be seriously reevaluated. Forty-eight hours is a lot of extra time, how is yours being spent? How much of this time being offered to God?

A prayerful state of mind should be the condition of every devoted Christian wherever they may be. Whether at the grocery store or on a crowded jet, all behavior should be of a nature to glorify God! However, people may think you are a little off-key, crazy, or even fanatical if you were to fall down on your knees and prayed for thirty minutes in the aisles of the store blocking shopping cart flow. This is not the kind of representation that GOD desires of the Christian. Everything representing HIM should be done decently and in order. Nevertheless, if the trial or whatever you may be going through demands that you fall on your knees at the store, or if you are impressed by the HOLY SPIRIT to do so, then follow HIS lead. **"Whether therefore ye eat, or drink, or whatsoever ye do, do all to the glory of GOD."** 1 Cor. 10:31

Keep also in mind it is prayer that changes things. With much prayer comes much power, with little prayer comes little power, and where there is no prayer, there is no power. **"Watch ye therefore, and pray always, that ye may be accounted worthy to escape all these things that shall come to pass, and to stand before the SON of man."** Lk 21:36

Prayer is the key to Christian devotion, and it is the means by which we come in contact with infinite resources. James said, **"Ye lust, and have not: ye kill, and desire to have, and cannot obtain; ye fight and war, yet ye have not, because ye ask not."** James 4:2 Again, the word of GOD says, **"Then shall ye call upon ME, and ye shall go and pray unto ME, and I will harken unto you."** Jer. 29:12 **"Watch and pray, that ye enter not into temptation: the spirit indeed is willing but the flesh is weak."** Matt. 26:41 There are many biblical references to prayer and why it is needed so much. Search the scriptures with prayer and find peace to your soul.

The main deterrence for temptation is prayer, and it also reveals a dependence on JESUS. With prayer, GOD sees the individual or group with a dependence on Him taking the matter before the throne room of grace not attempting to handle matters themselves. **"Confess your faults one to another, and pray one for another, that ye may be healed. The effectual fervent prayer of a righteous man availeth much."** James 5:16

Prayer with faith can move mountainous situations that are in the

Christian's life. It can heal the sick and deliver the captives. It is the chosen method by the Heavenly FATHER by which we lowly souls may communicate with HIM. Remember the story in Daniel chapter 2 when King Nebuchadnezzar was going to kill all the wise men because they could not interpret his dream? Daniel was included with them to be killed because he too was numbered with the wise men. When he heard about the decree and after requesting some time from the commander of the army that the king should give him and his friends a chance to consider the matter. Instead of those young men simply getting together and brainstorming to see how they could come up with good ideas to thwart the situation as do most organizations, they got together and went to GOD in prayer. **"Then Daniel went to his house, and made the thing known to Hananiah, Mishael, and Azariah, his companions: That they would desire mercies of the GOD of heaven concerning this secret; that Daniel and his fellows should not perish with the rest of the wise men of Babylon. Then was the secret revealed unto Daniel in a night vision. Then Daniel blessed the God of heaven."** Dan 2:20-22 Prayer is always key. How can an answer and a blessing to prayer be received if no prayer is offered up? During the reign of the Medes and Persians Daniel was caught praying three times a day after an imperial decree was passed that no one should ask any petition or request of any god or man except of the king and if caught doing so would be cast into a den of lions. Needless to say Daniel the man of God continued in prayer making his requests known unto God. He was thrown into the den of hungry lions but praise be to God he was delivered without a scratch. It is humble prayer that moves mountains, stop the mouths of lions, heal the sick, and increase spirituality.

THE LATTER CHURCH

By the time every apostle of CHRIST had suffered some form of persecution or killed, the church was already slipping into apostasy. Giving it some intuitive thought; the devil had already crept in on the twelve before CHRIST was crucified and left the earth. Consider Judas; he could not get any deeper into the church nor could he physically get any closer to JESUS. He sat right at the same dinner table with Jesus, and as can be imagined, he probably slept at times in the same company with the Lord. From a physical perspective, Judas was as close to Jesus as anyone could get, and this is the very reason why he was so easily able to know His comings/goings and to betray Him. **"And He answered and said, 'He that dippeth his hand with Me in the dish, the same shall betray Me.'"** Matt. 26:23

Like some self-proclaimed Christians today, Judas could have enjoyed a much closer spiritual walk with Jesus while he was in the church, but like so many, he chose not to. He had every opportunity to draw closer to CHRIST but did not. Like some churchgoers today, his heart only grew harder and harder. The Christian Church had just started up, and the devil had already joined! How many devils do you think are standing in the pulpits and sitting in the pews of congregations today? Satan is operating from more positions of any given local congregation than could possibly be imagined. Further evidence of this surfaced after the conversion, and while brother Paul walked the earth, he mentioned that the mystery of iniquity was working already in the church.

Keep in mind that this was while the Christian Church was just getting under way. It was in its infancy. **"For the mystery of iniquity doth already work:"** 2 Thess. 2 He was referring to iniquity working already in the church.

As time went on, the church began to slip further and further into darkness. Satan had so deceptively navigated himself up with skill through the ranks and actually was able to set at the head of the visible church. This was incorporated during the time period known through history as the Dark Ages. Even secular history testifies to the darkness of the then-known church by deeming it the Dark Ages.

It is important to keep in mind that the church in power during the Dark Ages was a persecuting church and evolved from the organized system of religious worship that JESUS left with the apostles. There is a striking similarity to the darkness of the Jewish church at the time of the birth of Christ and during His ministry as when the Dark Ages took effect. This church's evolution took place over a span of time and became known as the universal church. We know it today as the Catholic Church. But when the church reached the threshold of the Dark Ages, it was in complete apostasy and Satan had seized control of the entire organized structure through paganism and by giving the bishop of Rome empirical civil power along with ecclesiastical powers to set his seat at the head in the form of the papacy. **"And the beast which I saw was like a leopard, and his feet were as the feet of a bear, and his mouth of a lion: and the dragon gave him his power, and his seat, and great authority."** Rev. 13:2

The enemy of all righteousness (the devil) used men within the noticeable Christian Church (then known as the Roman Catholic Church) to openly persecute and kill true followers of CHRIST (Christians). Millions of true Christians died for the sake of a straight testimony. They were hunted and killed like wild animals by people who called themselves Christians. If the purity of the faith still exists and people are still living up to true Christian standards, then why isn't this same type of spiritual persecution taking place in the world today? Satan and his imps haven't taken a vacation! The question is "Are the Christian principles and standards being kept today as with the Christians of Acts 2 and the early church?" Why Christians today are not being hunted, persecuted, and killed as back then? Maybe it is because most are taking on a form of godliness but denying the powers thereof. **"Having a form of godliness but denying the power thereof: of such turn away."** 2 Tim. 3:5 (Even though there will come a time when even those who make a claim to be a follower of Jesus will be tested to see if their heart is where their mouth is, it is time to follow Christ according to the conscript of His Holy Word.)

Today, if there are one or two within a congregation even close to living up to what it means to be a true follower of GOD, they may not be being haunted and killed as such in the earlier days, but they are in the church being cast aside, derided, talked about, and looked down upon and in some cases dis-fellowshipped! And may end up being killed if they don't look out! But the devil saw, during the Dark Ages, that every time he and his little imps would martyr or kill a true Christian, many more would pop up in their places. Many of them died with smiles on their faces singing hymnals and good Christian songs while going to what seemed to be their demise. But actually, they were putting their trust in nail-scarred hands and the next voice they will hear is the sweet voice of Jesus calling them home. As did the early Christians, put your trust in JESUS when all hell breaks loose on you!

Many people saw these fellow believers standing strong in their faith going to their deaths singing about JESUS, and this was a witness to them. This caused many nonbelievers to seek out this JESUS and to be converted. They had never seen anyone die with smiles on their faces as the flames engulfed them or as they were tortured.

The enemy of all righteousness did not like what was going on. Something had to be done to prevent Christianity from spreading so rapidly. So the devil and his boys had a little imp convention (kind of like some church board meetings) and decided to instead of killing these Christians openly (in order to prevent true Christianity from multiplying) they would perform guerrilla warfare as they did when CHRIST and the first apostles walked the earth. That is, they would infiltrate the pure church by joining it and operate from within at all levels to attempt to tear down inside the walls and destroy what GOD had set up. Keep in mind that he had to recruit men, women, boys, and girls to carry out this plan and meet his objectives. The military today may have a harder time recruiting people for military service than the general of unrighteousness for the destruction of godly principles. He has people who willfully answer his call as soon as he bids them come. As he did to Judas, he could not carry out his devious plan without the aid of human agents to do it. It is high time that diligent inventory of the soul takes place and see which spiritual entity is truly being served in the heart and in the church! It can only be one of the two. **"For as many as are led by the Spirit of God, they are the sons of God."** Rom. 8:14 The enemy joins the ranks of true fellow believers and begins to take office, not to help in the cause of CHRIST but under the guise of Christianity to destroy. **"For such are false apostles, deceitful workers, transforming themselves into the apostles of CHRIST. And no marvel; for Satan himself is transformed into an angel of light."** Rev. 11:13 and 14

There are many smooth talkers and eloquent orators in the pulpits of today, but does that mean that they are truly of GOD because they have a degree and are standing in a pulpit? Absolutely not! JESUS HIMSELF said, **"Beware of false prophets, which come to you in sheep's clothing, but inwardly they are ravening wolves."** Matt. 7:15 This is to inform us not to be deceived with fanciful eloquent speakers but to follow a straight 'Thus saith the LORD!'

From a logical perspective, there are enemies standing in the pulpits of popular churches all across the land. One would have to be very naive to think otherwise. The word of God gives plenty of ground to stand on so as not to be ensnared by Satan. **"To the law and to the testimony, if they speak not according to this Word, it is because there is no light in them."** Isa. 8:20

All manner of false doctrines began to creep into the Christian Church. They begin to do like the nonbelieving Jews before them to teach for doctrine the commandments of men and to depart from the truth. **"Ye hypocrites, well did Esaias prophesy of you, saying, 'This people draweth nigh [near] unto ME with their mouth, and honoreth ME with their lips; but their heart is far from ME.' But in vain they do worship ME, teaching for doctrines the commandments of men."** Matt. 15:7–9

GOD always gives instruction and/or direction on how HE wants things done, but HE also gives us choices. HE does not force the conscience or the will of men. More times than not, it is sad to say, that man will either choose not to follow the LORD, or he will attempt to alter GOD's way somehow and mold them to fit his own desires and lifestyle or the lifestyle of popular beliefs. This is the most dangerous spiritual course to take because when this happens, the more comfortable you can get in your sins not realizing that it is part of the adversary's plan to mislead, hinder, and destroy, even though the church may appear to be prospering financially. No matter how you slice it, it goes against GOD and will guarantee you a first-class seat on the vessel torpedoing straight for hell!

Fact is, many people believe that they are on the right track, but if they will truly take inventory of themselves while humbly seeking to exchange self-will for GOD's unalterable will, they are sure to find there is plenty of room for improvement. It really is a simple procedure, recognized as getting rid of self or putting self aside. **"Humble yourselves therefore under the mighty hand of GOD, that HE may exalt you in due time: Casting all your care upon HIM; for HE careth for you. Be sober be vigilant; because your adversary the devil, as a roaring lion, walketh about, seeking whom he may devour."** 1 Pet. 5:6–8

The latter church developed some serious problems for all who attempted substituting GOD's way for man's way. If any tried to teach a straight doctrinal message instead of for doctrine the commandments of men, they were dealt with immediately. The Dark Ages brought in much persecution and death for many Christians who followed a straight "Thus saith the LORD." The Dark Ages, as foretold in scripture (see and study the 2,300-day prophecy of Daniel 8) lasted approximately 1,260 years. At the end of this 1,260-year period mentioned in the prophetic books of Daniel and Revelation as time, times, and dividing of time, 42 months, and time, times, and a half time, all are referring to the same prophetic time period of 1,260 years that the Dark Age period engulfed. Around the end of this time period, GOD shed some light in the Dark Ages on a man of the then-known persecuting church by the name of Martin Luther. Much like Paul who was of the persecuting church when he too was called by God to serve Him. Martin Luther was a preacher for the church that had ultimately left off serving the LORD as JESUS and the apostles had instituted.

Most of them of the faith during this time were as it is today thinking that they were serving the LORD in HIS truest light. But they failed to search for the LORD with all their heart. They were dogmatized and taught what they assumed was apparent truth and fail to study for themselves. In other words, they were being spoon-fed sound good sugar coated lies. To accept what is taught from the pulpit or any institution without self-investigation is a *great* danger because it is human nature to go against GOD, and men will do so when given the chance. They will teach what sounds and feels good to them and maybe support it by misinterpreting one text. Once fallacy creeps in and is accepted, it will continue on that path until more fallacy is instituted. As more and more fallacies are accepted by the institution, the more difficult it will be for it to stop and get back on track with God. Hardly ever do accepted fallacy returns back to right practices. Though it may feel good, sound good, taste and smell good . . . if it is going against God's plan, it is going the wrong way! Humans will naturally follow the course of sin if left unchecked by the HOLY SPIRIT. **"And ye shall seek ME, and find ME, when ye shall search for ME with all your heart."** Jer. 29:13 Diligent search for the Almighty's way must take place before He can be found! **"And ye shall seek Me, and find Me, when ye shall search for Me with all your heart."** Jer. 29:13

Furthermore, the admonition is given by God to, **"Study to show thyself approve unto GOD, a workman that needth not to be ashamed, rightly dividing the WORD of truth."** 2 Tim. 2:15 It is not enough to simply go to the church building and then make the claim, "I know that I am a child of God, because I go to church every time the doors are open." The time has come and is far spent for every believer to "study with prayer to show themselves approved unto God."

You cannot leave it up to an organization or some systematical procedures to see you into the kingdom of GOD. You must have a direct one-on-one relationship with the SAVIOR. Organization and structure is good and may well have been instituted by GOD, but it is composed of men, and this is where fault is found. Hitler's armies were well-organized and structured, but look at the hellrific terror and damage his demonic forces assailed upon the world. So just because there is organization and structure does not mean it is of God.

The institution is good, the structure of man faulty. Therefore, because there is an element of fault (man) incorporated into the system of worship which may play on your salvation, it is imperative that you look up to and directly toward JESUS and not to men. Keep your eyes upon Jesus! The enemy of all righteousness will often attempt to alter the plans of how he deceives you, but the objective is still the same to keep you out of heaven and God's glory. He is with high levels of deception, diligently attempting to invoke all of GOD's children into hell with him. Therefore, the same deceptions he used all through history are still being used by him today only with various modifications pertaining to the times in which he deceives. He does not have to use any new thing because man's lusts are essentially unchanged throughout the course of time. The most common of these are money or material wealth, things pertaining to the flesh (as sex), power, and pride along with lies.

Therefore, if you commit to the error of following men as opposed to focusing on JESUS, you will fall prey to any of the falsehoods that plagued the church preceding and during the Dark Ages. If you are undecided about something that is spiritual and the thing may have some impact on where you spend eternity and you do not know which way to turn, do not make the mistake of turning to men; turn to JESUS! There is hope in none other! **"To whom GOD would make known what is the riches of the glory of this mystery among the gentiles; which is Christ in you, the hope of glory: Whom we preach, warning every man, and teaching every man in all wisdom; that we may present every man <u>perfect in CHRIST JESUS</u>."** Col. 1:27 and 28

Please keep in mind that there are not too many people who will lead you to heaven, but there are a whole mess of folk who will take you by the hand and lead you straight to hell! That is, if you let them! They are not going in themselves to heaven, and they do not want to see you get there either! Look at what JESUS told some of these higher-ups in the church of HIS day, **"For ye have taken away the key of knowledge: Ye enter not in yourselves, and them that were entering in ye hindered."** Lk 11:52 Please be advised and be certain that no one mislead you, hinder you, or steer you anything opposite of a straight "Thus saith the LORD" and a straight testimony. And the most promising way of doing that is to "study to show yourself approved before God" with prayer. **"To the law and to the testimony, if they speak not according to this Word: it is because it is no light in them."** Isa. 8:20

GOD used a man by the name of Martin Luther to begin a reformation and protest against what the world recognized as the then-known church. He eventually, after much persecution, ridicule, and sensor by the leaders of the then-known church, nailed ninety-five thesis on the church door in Wittenberg, Germany, outlining how off course the church was and how they had become entrenched in doctrines and philosophies that had nothing to do with the teachings of God but followed the commandments of men. Placing these thesis on the church doors there in Germany begun what we know of today as the Great Reformation. And from this great reform movement, Protestantism was born. (Again the scope of this book is not to give the entire Protestant movement account but to lead the reader to a deeper understanding of Christianity and the need for prayerful study.)

The birth of Protestantism (not to be confused with the Reformation; they are two separate events) actually took place when the princes of Squires protested against the imperialism of popery and the Catholic Church based on the teachings of Martin Luther who started the Reformation. Every so-called Christian church (whether real or unreal) in existence today that is not of the Catholic faith is under the general heading of Protestantism. The term means that of protesting. That is protesting against the then-known Catholic Church, the only recognizable church of its day. With the dawning of this new light, immediately, the powers of darkness went into action. And by virtue of Satan, Protestantism, with the use of the human factor during this time, evolved into many different factions or denominations. Remember it is declared by the WORD of GOD, **"One Lord, one faith, and one baptism."** **Eph. 4:5** So the enemy decided to add confusion during this delicate time period of transformation by adding error to truth by substituting the concept of "one Lord, one faith, and one baptism" to one Lord (Jesus), many faiths (many denominations), and many baptisms (many different baptisms). Can you see how this would over time cause much confusion not only in the church but in the world also?

However, it is the solemn duty of every professed Christian, wherever you are and whichever denomination you may be associated with, to seek out GOD's truth with much prayer and find the true faction of this Protestant movement or in other words the straight and narrow way. There is and logically always will be **ONE TRUE FAITH.** It follows logic because there is only one wise God. And if there is only one God, then it stands to reason that there should only be one true faith and one true belief. Therefore, the seeker of truth will follow the path of logically eliminating all elements that are not meticulously following God's word and will eventually be led to the only one true church. **"There is <u>one</u> body, and <u>one</u> SPIRIT, even as you are called in <u>one</u> hope of your calling; <u>One</u> LORD, <u>one</u> faith, and <u>one</u> baptism, <u>one</u> GOD and FATHER of all, who is above all, and through all, and in you all."** Eph. 4:4–6 Amen!

That is, all who are living by the will of God and therefore living in CHRIST JESUS will, with much effort, seek to enter at the straight gate for JESUS Himself said, **"Enter ye in at the strait gate: for wide is the gate, and broad is the way, that leadeth to destruction, and many there be which go in thereat: Because strait is the gate, and narrow is the way, which leadeth unto life, and few there be that find it."** Matt. 7:13 and 14

Keep searching by faithful prayer with all your heart the LORD will lead you in the right direction and to the true baptismal fount. This is the hope of your calling. **"Then ye shall call upon ME, and ye shall go and pray unto ME, and I will harken unto you. And ye shall seek ME, and find ME, when ye shall search for ME with all your heart."** Jer. 29:12 and 13 The text does not say to search for Him with some diluted part of your heart, but it says to search for Him with all (100 percent) of your heart and you will find Him.

Within this earthly test-tube experience, you will find at least two very distinct groups of people. As it was in the early church, the true Christians were very distinct in their deportment and their worship, even to the point of them being noticeably observed and hunted by emperors, high priest, and other high-ranking officials of the day. How else could these lowly Christians have been singled out and hunted like wild animals by so-called higher-ups? The Christians were different. They did not look like the world, talk like the world, nor worship like those who sought their lives. **"But ye are a chosen generation, a royal priesthood, a holy nation, a peculiar people; that ye should show forth the praises of Him who hath called you out of darkness into His marvelous light."** 1 Pet. 2:9

Though many examples can be used to illustrate this point, the following one will be used to demonstrate the lack of a fundamental difference between nominal Christians and the world today. In other words, there should be only two groups of people in the world relative to God: those who follow Him and those who do not. Those who follow Him should be believing Christians, and those who do not should be categorized as non-Christian. There is, however, a third group—those who claim to be Christian but are not following God at His word. This group can actually be categorized with the non-Christians because they may go to church and behave piously but hardly live a true Christian life.

For example, at Christmastime, even though no one knows for sure exactly what day our Lord and Savior Jesus Christ was born, Christians, as well as the secular world, recognize or believe that December 25 is the day of His birth. While at the shopping malls at Christmastime, there is a very high volume of shopping not on spiritualistic goods but on contrast there is a high level of focus on materialistic goods. On Black Friday (the day immediately following Thanksgiving and the official day that Christmas shopping begins), it is on record that people have been pepper-sprayed, stampeded, beaten up, shot, yes, and even killed, all in the name of the birth of Christ. How sickening?

The two groups the self-proclaimed Christians and non-Christians are not indistinguishable at the shopping malls. There would be no noticeable difference between the Godly and ungodly when there in fact should be. They are engaged in exactly the same worldly traffic and consumerism, all in the name of the birth of the Messiah. You know the old saying if it walks like a duck, acts like a duck, and quacks like a duck, then it must be a duck! If they shop like the world, dress like the world, and act like the world, then they must be of the world! **"Love not the world, neither the things that are in the world. If any man loves the world, the love of the Father is not in him."** 1 John 2:15 They proclaim to be Christians when they are in essence behaving and following the same practices of the non-Christian: chasing after the same worldly materialistic goods, getting deeper into debt, and not following Christ at all. Truth be told, true Christians should not even be at the malls during this time, unless they are there for the purposes of soul winning or working for the Lord. Because most things being sought after at this time has absolutely nothing to do with Christ or His birth. Practices of the true Christian would only continue at Christmastime what they have been practicing all year: visiting the sick, helping the needy, visiting them that are in prison, etc. Doing Godly deeds not just one day out of the year but all year long doing those things that Jesus said to do. Not only on December 25 but as often as you can every day of the year. "**When the Son of man shall come in His glory, and all the holy angels with Him, then shall He sit upon the throne of His glory. And before Him shall be gathered all nations, and He shall separate them one from another, as a shepherd divideth His sheep from the goats. And He shall set the sheep on His right hand, but the goats on the left. Then shall the King say unto them on His right hand, 'Come, ye blessed of My Father, inherit the kingdom prepared for you from the foundation of the world. For I was an hungered, and ye gave me meat; I was thirsty, and ye gave me drink; I was a stranger, and ye took Me in: Naked, and ye clothe Me; I was sick, and ye visited Me; I was in prison, and ye came unto Me'. Then shall the righteous answer, Him saying, Lord, when saw we Thee a hungered, and fed Thee or thirsty, and gave Thee drink? When saw we Thee a stranger, and took Thee in? Or naked, and clothed Thee? Or when saw we Thee sick, or in prison, and came unto Thee? And the King shall answer and say unto them, 'Verily, I say unto you, inasmuch as ye have done it unto one of the least of these my brethren, ye have done it unto Me'. Then shall He say also unto them on the left hand, 'Depart from Me, ye cursed, unto everlasting fire, prepared for the devil and his angels. For I was an hungered, and ye gave Me no meat, I was thirsty, and ye gave Me no drink; I was a stranger, and ye took Me not in, naked, and ye clothed Me not; sick, and in prison, and ye visited Me not.' Then shall** they also answer Him, saying, 'Lord, when saw we Thee an hungered, or athirst, or a stranger, or naked, or sick, or in prison, and did not minister unto Thee?' Then shall He answer them, saying, 'Verily I say unto you, Inasmuch as ye did it not to one of the least of these, ye did it not to Me.' And these shall go away into everlasting punishment; but the righteous into life eternal." Matt. 25:31–46

According to the above texts, Jesus never said to visit the malls and He did *not* tell us His birthday! As a matter of fact, in all four gospels, Jesus's death and resurrection is emphasized more than His birth. His death and resurrection signified the importance as to why He came into this world, His love for us, and the devastating power of sin. This is the only event He Himself memorialized by the breaking of bread and drinking the fruit of the vine, that night when He was betrayed, took bread, " **And when He had given thanks, he brake it, and said, 'Take eat: this is My body, which is broken for you: this do in <u>remembrance</u> of Me.' After the same manner also He took the cup, when He had supped, saying, 'This cup is the new testament in My blood: this do ye, as oft as ye drink it, in <u>remembrance</u> of Me.' For as often as ye eat this bread, and drink this cup, ye do show the Lord's death till He come.' Wherefore whosoever shall eat this bread, and drink this cup of the Lord, unworthily, shall be guilty of the body and blood of the Lord."** 1 Cor. 11:24–27

Please take note, so-called end-time Christians follow after the world with unprecedented zeal, but the things that Christ said to do are hardly ever done. Why is that? Why are worldly practices and activities so easily followed when the things of Christ are slighted and difficult for the modern-day Christians to do? Ask yourself, my fellow Christian, when was the last time you visited some stranger who was sick? Or some stranger who is under the oppressive detriment of the law?

Because the topic of Christmas was used in the previous example, let us take a little closer look at what we call Jesus's birthday.

The account of the birth of our Savior Jesus Christ was given only in explicit detail by the gospel of Luke. The gospel of Matthew mentions His birth but only briefly, and the other two gospels of Mark and John omitted it altogether. The Messiah just shows up as prophesied.

However, even in the gospel of Luke with much detail of the circumstances surrounding the Messiah's birth, the exact date of His birth is omitted. It is never mentioned! If Jesus's birthday was of such great importance, would not an almighty God, in His infinite wisdom, give us an exact date? Maybe it should be avoided altogether simply because it is a man-made and not a God-made celebration. (Again, "Teaching for doctrine the commandments of men.")

Once the information of the Savior's birth by the Virgin Mary is given in the gospels, no aspect of that birth is ever mentioned again anywhere within the sacred scriptures. Not by God the Father, God the Son, nor by God the Holy Spirit; not by His earthly parents Mary or Joseph; nor by any of His apostles, prophets, or disciples. Surely a holiday celebration so recognized by the entire world and so extremely commercialized and of such materialistic magnitude, if it were that important for us to know and to follow, should not it had been mentioned again by some entity or representative of righteousness? God never gave it to us!

Santa Claus and Christmas trees, with all the trimmings and toys, are placed on youngsters at such an early age that it leaves such an indelible impression on the mind; department stores continue to use these icons on them after they become adults! When they place Santa Claus in advertisements and on their store windows, it is not for the children. Children do not have the kind of money they are trying to get. It is the adults being lured by these iconic images placed on them with such meticulous care by worldliness from their youth up that it can hardly be shunned. The adults who were once children where these highly impressionable lies have been placed upon are the ones sought after to buy the worldly merchandise, and it is a continual adult-to-child cycle that takes place from year to year. Please be aware of how easy it is to get caught up in worldliness without even being aware of it! This is only one small facet of modern-day Christian behavioral conduct under observation here. There are many more that could be placed under the spiritual microscope.

One other observation though worth mentioning at this point concerning not only Christ's birth date (which no one really knows for sure) but all birthdays considered in the Bible. You may be well-informed that from a biblical perspective, the word *birthday* is only mentioned on two occasions throughout the entire Bible. From the book of Genesis to the book of Revelation, the word *birthday* is never mentioned concerning any man of God, angel, prophet, priest, God-fearing king, or any other entity associated with righteousness. Zero! None! On both occasions where the word *birthday* is mentioned in scripture, it is associated only with two men who were in opposition to God: (1) the pharaoh, king of Egypt who was the direct descendant of pharaoh that killed the children of God in a vain attempt to murder baby Moses (God's deliverer for ancient Israel), and (2) the direct descendant of Herod, king of Israel who likewise killed the babies of God's children in a vain attempt to murder baby Jesus (God's present-day deliverer of Israel). Notice how these two occurrences of such similarity repeated themselves in biblical history many hundreds of years apart. They are almost of the exact magnitude of each other, and it is interesting to note that they both were descendants of baby killers of those attempting to follow God. These are the only two times for these two ungodly men the word *birthday* is mentioned in the entire word of God. Satan, my friend, is after your children. Birthday celebrations are dangerous not only in church but altogether dangerous. They sort of imply that you were somehow the author of your own birth. "Happy birthday to YOU" are songs sung at a very early age incriminating the young mind. This song can have a simple alteration to give glory to God singing it with the same tune as happy birthday to you. "Thank God for you; Thank God for you;" and the second stanza can go like this: "May Jesus bless you; May Jesus bless you;" **"And it came to pass the third day, which was pharaoh's *birthday*, that he made a feast unto all his servants:"** Gen. 40:20 Also, **"And when a convenient day was come, that Herod on his *birthday* made a supper to his lords, high captains, and chief estates of Galilee."** Mk 6:21 Remember that these two men were direct descendants of baby killers. Why then are birthdays held in such a high regard today when the celebration itself does not appear to be ordained by God? Why is December 25 held in such a high regard today not only in the world but in the Christian churches as well? Also, the birthdays of pastors and church members are often elevated during worship services nowadays when only God should be obtaining any and all glory at all times, let alone during the worship services. Amen. Is there any wonder why churches are in spiritual decay and spiraling out of control?

The latter-day church in this test tube is far off track, and every attempt with great effort should be made to get it back on track to the edification and glorification of God. Not everyone who claims to be a child of God will enter the kingdom of God. And they could very well be going to church every time the church doors open and still be in the non-saved category. Jesus admonishes, **"Not everyone that saith unto Me, Lord, Lord shall enter into the kingdom of heaven; but he that doeth the will of My Father which is in heaven. Many will say to Me in that day, Lord, Lord, have we not prophesied in Thy name? And in Thy name have cast out devils? And in Thy name done many wonderful works? And then will I profess unto them, I never knew you: depart from Me, ye that work iniquity."** Matt. 7:21-23

It is important to recognize here that Jesus is referring to church folk, not world-lings! The latter-day church for the most part needs to make a drastic turn around. To get out of its comfort zone and get back to a straight thus saith the LORD! **"Thus saith the Lord, 'Stand ye in the ways, and see, and ask for the old paths, where is the good way, and walk therein,** and ye shall find rest for your souls;' But they said, 'We will not walk therein.'" Jer. 6:16

Take a closer look at the contrasting differences between the early Christian Church and modern or latter churches. We saw the graphical representation where Jesus was at the head of and working with His early church by way of the Holy Spirit; most of today's churches are working under other influences such as greed and monetary gain.

In the organizational structure of some of the present-day churches diagram, you can see that though they may proclaim Jesus with their mouths; in actuality, it is not He at the head. There are no true connections to the Lord.

{Latter-day churches organizational structure}may include

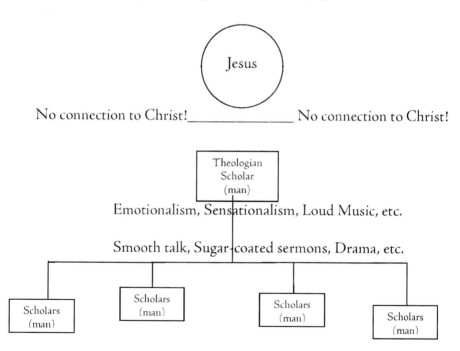

Also, it may be noted that the rectangular shapes represent various church sizes from not so large congregations to megachurches. The larger the congregation is usually an indication of the leadership's ability to speak smooth things and to woo a crowd.

Please remember that God's true church will unnoticeably continue forward in these latter days as the church did during the Dark Ages. It will consist of people that most would not think are a part of this true church. God doesn't see as man sees. For man looks at the outward appearance, but God sees the heart as mentioned in the book of Samuel. This group of people will therefore make up the true church that has existed since the beginning of time and is in essence the church that Christ is coming to receive upon His second coming. **"That He might present to Himself a glorious church, not having spot, or wrinkle; or any such thing; but that it should be holy and without blemish."** Eph. 5:27

One quick and simple self-check to see if you will make up a part of this true church or not is to apply the Romans 8:4–14 self-tester. If you are one of those who go to church week after week but your mind is primarily on the things of this world that is of the flesh, then there is a good chance that you will not be one of the lambs that Christ is coming back for, **"That the righteousness of the law might be fulfilled in us, who walk not after the flesh, but after the Spirit. For they that are after the flesh do mind the things of the flesh; but they that are after the Spirit the things of the Spirit. For to be carnally minded is death; but to be Spiritually minded is life and peace. Because the carnal mind is enmity against God: for it is not subject to the law of God, neither indeed can be. So then they that are in the flesh cannot please God. But ye are not in the flesh, but in the Spirit, if so be that the Spirit of God dwell in you. Now if any man have not the Spirit of Christ, he is none of His. And if Christ be in you, the body is dead because of sin; but the Spirit is life because of righteousness. But if the Spirit of Him that raised up Christ from the dead shall also quicken your mortal bodies by His Spirit do mortify the deeds of the body, ye shall live. <u>For as many as are led by the Spirit of God, they are the sons of God.</u>"** Rom. 8:4–14

The Second Coming of Jesus
and
God's True Church

At Jesus' second coming to this world that we are conceptualizing as a test tube, it will be literal, eventful, and momentous. It will not be a secret rapture as many believe, and it will by no means be a quiet event. **"For as the lightning cometh out of the east, and shineth even unto the west; so shall also the coming of the Son of man be."** Matt. 24:27 And also, **"The earth shall reel to and fro like a drunkard, and shall be removed like a cottage;"** Isa. 24:20

When Jesus comes back with the very distinguishable loud voice of the archangel, every eye shall see Him, every tongue shall confess, and every knee will bow to Him. He is coming back in the majestic splendor of all His glory! And the entire heavenly host comes back with Him. **"When the Son of Man shall come in His glory, and all the holy angels with Him, then shall He sit upon the throne of His glory."** Matt. 25:31

When His return becomes imminent and no longer a hope but a reality for the redeemed, the testing period will have long been over. There are no more tests to be done! The final exams have taken place. The eternal fate of every single individual that has ever lived within this test-tube domain is forever fixed and sealed before Christ's return. All who have continued not only in open sins and rebellion (non-Christians) but also those who claim to be Christians but has consistently not followed Christ at His Word but sought after the desires of their own lusts. Though He has beckoned them time after time, they have trusted in their own way. **"This know also, that in the last days perilous times shall come. For men shall be lovers of their own selves, covetous, boasters, proud, blasphemers, disobedient to parents, unthankful, unholy; Without natural affection, trucebreakers, false accusers, incontinent, fierce, despisers of those that are good; Traitors, heady, high-minded, lovers of pleasures more than lovers of GOD."** 2 Tim. 3:1–4

Those who have selfishly followed their own inclinations and desires, who refused to keep the word of God and to submit unto His will, also will not take part in the blessings that He has in store for those who **"Keep the commandments of God and have the testimony of Jesus Christ."** Rev. 12:17 Only those who consistently adhere to the will and word of God and follow Him at His word, they will make it through to behold His Glory and be partakers of it. **"He that is unjust, let him be unjust still: and he which is filthy, let him be filthy still: and he that is righteous, let him be righteous still: and he that is holy, let him be holy still."** Rev. 22:11 **"And grieve not the Holy Spirit of God, whereby ye are sealed unto the day of redemption."** Eph. 4:30

You will be either sealed unto redemption or you will be sealed to destruction. There is no middle ground. Again, those who will be found worthy to take part in His second coming and resurrection will comprise only those who will make up the true church of God at the day of His appearing. As the true Christians were of Paul's day the people who make up the true church of God are not readily seen. **"Let both grow together until the harvest: and in the time of the harvest I will say to the reapers, 'Gather ye together first the tares, and bind them in bundles to burn them: but gather the wheat into My barn."** Matt. 13:30

The Bible declares that the wheat and tares must grow together. Therefore, the representative church here on earth is comprised of those who will make it into heaven, the wheat, and those who will not, the tares. Christ is the gardener; He does the weeding! His angels are the reapers, and those that are harvested as the wheat make up the true church of God. **"Blessed and holy is he that take part in the first resurrection: on such the second death hath no power, but they shall be priests of God and of Christ, and shall reign with Him a thousand years."** Rev. 20:6

All peoples from Adam's day to this present day and every day in between, to the time of His return, all who do the will of God will participate in this glorious event. Stumbling into heaven because of your church affiliation or because of what your name or title is will not happen. It will not matter in that day how many letters of the alphabet that is in front of or behind your name (PhDs, MDs, EdDs, DMDs, honorary titles, etc.). It won't matter how many degrees you have! What will matter in that day is if you followed God by doing the things He said to do. You must have a right to behold and enter into the city. **"Blessed are they that do His commandments that they may have a right to the tree of life, and enter in through the gates into the city."** Rev. 22:14

God's true church today consists of all people who are seeking to follow righteousness and truth, not by denominational titles, creeds, or points of view, but by whosoever do the will of God. Jesus says, **"For whosoever shall do the will of God, the same is My brother, and My sister, and mother."** Mk 3:35 Jesus our Lord admonishes us to believe in Him, to obey His voice, and to be perfect by adhering to His Father's word. **"My sheep hear My voice, and I know them, and they follow Me."** Jn. 10:27 And also, **"Be ye therefore perfect, even as your Father which is in heaven is perfect."** Matt. 5:48

In other words, you may not as of yet belong to any denomination or group of religious followers, but you have a love to do right and have a deep love for truth. You are not far from the kingdom of GOD already. With much seeking, studying, and prayer, God will lead you to His true church where you can abide until His second coming. **"And ye shall seek Me, and** find Me, when ye shall search for Me with *all* your heart." Jer. 29:13 No matter who you are or where you are, if there is a strong sincere desire for truth and seeking of God, He may be found.

At the present time, there are hundreds, if not thousands, of different denominations listed under the general heading of Protestant Christian churches in the United States alone. This is a huge problem here with so many different denominations because the scriptures clearly teach us that there is one place to abide until our Lord comes back. **"There is one body, and one Spirit, even as ye are called in one hope of your calling, One Lord, one faith, one baptism."** Eph. 4:4 and 5

Since the beginning of time, God has had a true church and a true following even if it consisted of only one man (Adam), or of only one family (Noah and his family). God has sheep throughout all the earth, and God has sheep in various localities the church is unaware of. There are sheep in other parts of the world that do not even know that they are sheep, and there are lost sheep everywhere. This is an important reason why the gospel must go forward to the entire world. To every corner of the earth, the Gospel of Christ must go forward. However, it will not carry itself! This is why all believers must work while it is still day. For the night cometh when no man can work. **"All power is given unto me in heaven and in earth. Go ye therefore, and teach all nations, baptizing them in the name of the Father, and of the Son, and of the Holy Ghost: Teaching them to observe all things whatsoever I have commanded you; and, lo, I am with you always, even unto the end of the world. Amen!"** Matt. 28:18–20

It is important for the true Shepherd (Jesus Christ) to bring all true Christians (children of God) into one fold. He is gathering in His flock from every corner of the world and once this is done, it is finished! **"And other sheep I have which are not of this fold; them also I must bring, and they shall hear my voice; and there shall be one fold, and one Shepherd."** John 10:16

The true church of God's followers are of this fold that Jesus has set up since the foundation of the world. Unlike popular beliefs, there is not a collection of individualized folds. This is what the enemy of all righteousness would have you to believe as part of his way to keep confusion in the earth. And all who willingly follow his confusions are children of his. **"Ye are of your father the devil, and the lusts of your father ye will do. He was a murderer from the beginning, and abode not in the truth, because there is no truth in him. When he speaketh a lie, he speaketh of his own: for he is a liar, and the father of it."** John 8:44

The word of God tells His children, His people, "To come out of her." He is simply telling them to come out of false doctrine and false religious beliefs. **"And I heard another voice from heaven, saying, Come out of her, My people, that ye be not partakers of her sins, and that ye receive not of her plagues."** Rev. 18:4

Another analogy or illustration will be given at this time in an attempt to present a clearer picture of what has happened throughout the ages, and it may also point out how so many denominations surfaced over the years. If intelligent thought is given on the subject, it does not make any sense for a single Godhead with sovereignty over one universe to have thousands of different avenues to perpetuate His Gospel and more are cropping up periodically as men are able to do so. Remember "One Lord one faith and one baptism as mentioned in Ephesians chapter 4." **"For God is not the author of confusion, but of peace, as in all churches of the saints."** 1 Cor. 14:13 Again when all churches of the saints are mentioned here it is not referring to multiple denominations. Because this was written by brother Paul in about 59AD we all know that there was only one Christian faith and practice at this time. Therefore when he says, "In all churches of the saints" he is referring to one faith and belief of many congregations in as many different localities.

If confusion arises within any aspect of determining God's true way or what is required of us in the following of Christ, *it is not of God!* It must therefore then be of the arch deceiver and the father of lies, Satan. **"He hath** shewed thee, O man, what is good; and what doth the LORD require of thee, but to do justly, and to love mercy, and to walk humbly with thy God." Mic. 6:8

Think about it for a moment; would God deliberately generate so much confusion within the Christian world that people would not know which denomination is the right one and simply follow their own agendas? Would God have it that a person who at any moment in time might be ready to leave worldliness and holistically ready to turn to Him, would first have to search out the truth through a maze of lies and falsehoods because of so many different denominations? With a God of perfect order it does not make any sense, and it is not probable that God would do that. If you think about it, it should be exactly the same as it was in Paul's day, when a person is ready to leave worldliness and turn to God, it should be a very simple matter and one church to turn to not thousands of different faiths and beliefs. It should not be like shopping for a pair of shoes with thousands of selections to choose from. There should be only one place to go when you are ready to give your heart to the Lord. As a matter of fact, according to the infallible scriptures, it should be as God planned. It is factual that God did not generate confusion within His own ranks! That would not make any sense whatsoever, and it certainly would not reflect an all-knowing and all-seeing straightway God.

You hear generalizations from men saying things like "God has many different avenues to His kingdom." and "One destination but many different ways of getting there!" Quotations like these by men may sound good, but they are given only to justify a continuation on the wrong paths by them. Quotes like these are of the archenemy because they are not the truth and will lead you only to one way; damnation, that is if the ultimate choice is to stay on the wrong pathway. Take heed, people of God, the Lord said, *"one way, one Lord, and one baptism!" Not thousands!*

This point can be further illustrated by the old "needle in a haystack" analogy.

NEEDLE IN A HAYSTACK ANALOGY

The expression "That's like looking for a needle in a haystack." Exemplifies the idea that you are seeking something very difficult to find or something very hard to do. The analogy is not saying the needle cannot be found; it is simply implying that whatever it is you are looking for would be tremendously difficult to find or next to impossible to find. Using this simple analogy in view of our discussion, the needle will represent *truth*, and the *word of God* and the hay represent *lies* by the *words of the father of lies*. Also notice that there is only one needle (one truth) and much hay (many lies) represented in the analogy which signify God's truth as opposed to the many lies told and spread by Satan.

In the Garden of Eden, at the very beginning, there was only one truth (the needle) and one lie (one strand of hay). God told Adam and Eve not to eat from the tree in the midst of the garden, the tree of knowledge of good and evil. God said, "The day you eat from it you would surely die" (the truth, represented by the needle). Then here comes old slew foot the devil and tells Eve, "Go ahead and eat the fruit and that you would not surely die"—the first recorded lie in scripture (the lie, represented by a strand of hay). The strand of hay (the lie) is placed over the needle (the truth) to distort and obscure it.

Notice there has always been one truth—*God's word!* On the other hand, over time, the devil has been continuously, purposely, and consistently adding more lies and deceptions (more and more hay) in an attempt to distort or cover up God's word (the truth) more. The more hay placed over the needle, the more obscure and the more difficult it is to find the truth, and He knows that. Over time the truth becomes so hidden that it would appear almost not to exist. People may come to believe anything that sounds good, looks good, smell good, and feels good, but it's a good chance it is not the truth. By these distorted truths, many have fallen to and are comfortable in the fallacies that have been accepted as truth. **"Even him, whose coming is after the working of Satan with all power and signs and lying wonders; and with all deceivableness of unrighteousness in them that perish; because they received not the love of the truth, that they might be saved. And for this cause God shall send them strong delusion, that they should believe a lie: that they all might be damned who believed not the truth, but had pleasure in unrighteousness."** 2 Thess.2: 9–12

It is the cardinal nature of man to want to hear sweet sugarcoated lies and not change their ways to the truth! Now with all this hay (lies) covering the needle (the truth), has the truth disappeared? Just by looking, it almost appears to be gone for good, but it has not! It is still there underneath and/ or mixed in with all of the hay (the lies).

Being absolutely clear on the subject, Satan would love to do away with God's word altogether, but he is unable to do so. He has tried many times to eradicate the message of salvation to man by a loving and caring God throughout the ages but has failed. He does not have the power to obliterate God's truth (otherwise, it would be completely wiped out), but the power is in him to deceive and obscure or block the WORD. Remember, he is the catalyst to hinder righteousness and promote wickedness. He is allowed to use every means available of his cunning arts and schemes to distort it, confuse it, and hide it as much as he is able for the purposes of deception. His primary motive is to deceive and cause people to follow him and ultimately to be lost! So since he cannot eradicate God's Word altogether he has introduced all manner of versions of the Word some with greater distortions than others and there are always misinterpretations of scripture for the down casting of souls. Whether people are conscientiously or ignorantly following him, his main goal is to get the wayward and the non-wayward to go against GOD and to get them destroyed as is the case with him. Remember, hell fire is really set by God for Satan and his imps, but all who refuse to accept and follow Christ will end up in there with them. **"Then shall He say also unto them on the left hand, 'Depart from Me, ye cursed, into everlasting fire, prepared for the devil and his angels.'"** Matt. 24:41

He is allowed to perform these strong deceptions simply because man has the power of choice. If he could destroy the word of God, then that would make him more powerful than GOD, and the human race would not have a choice or a chance! We could only follow the lie he puts before us and by the same token; if the devil did not have the opportunity to confuse the truth, man would only have the truth before him and simply follow it. GOD however, gave mankind a choice. Then let the truth be chosen and followed by mankind with all subjection and humility into the kingdom of God. Amen.

As man continues to traverse down through the corridors of time, as is the case today, the truth is just that much more difficult to find than it was in the early church's days. With all the lies and game playing with the word of God over the years, people have become disillusioned from the truth and in some cases disassociated with it altogether. A lot of people have become so disillusioned and accepting of all the *hocus pocus* that is being preached and taught today that they do not even want to hear a **'STRAIGHT THUS SAITH THE LORD'** anymore. They would be ready to eliminate the message and the messenger in order to continue in their deceptive designer religions.

Due to the times in which we live, a great number of people do not want to hear the truth or a straight testimony any more. Today, lies are preferred over the truth, wanting to hear something watered down or sugarcoated! They want to hear things that tickle the ear sounding good and eloquent. **"For the time will come when** *they will not endure sound doctrine;* **but after their own lusts shall they heap to themselves teachers, having itching ears; And they shall turn away their ears from the truth, and shall be turned unto fables."** 2 Tim. 4:3 and 4

The scriptures do not say they **cannot** endure but says, "**They will not endure!**" **"Speaking lies in hypocrisy; having their conscience seared with a hot iron."** 1 Tim. 4:2 **"And for this cause God shall send them strong delusion, that they should believe a lie; That they all might be damned who believed not the truth, but had pleasure in unrighteousness."** 2 Thess. 2:11 and 12

Face it, folks, many people are following after their own likes and dislikes not following God's way at all. **They want a designer religion!** They do not want to be moved out of their comfort zones, instead of a commitment to following a straight thus saith the Lord! Because studying the word of God with much prayer for truth is being slighted, most people do not really know what to believe or to trust and have a tendency to follow only smooth things or those things that sound good. The practices and sermons men create that cater to their preconceived religious beliefs and excitements. This is what is being followed! **"Which say to the seers, See not; and to the prophets, Prophesy not unto us right things,** *but* **speak unto us smooth things, prophesy deceits."** Isa. 30:10

Nevertheless, until the end of time, the truth is what it has always been, and God admonishes for it to be sought out and found. **"And ye shall seek me, and find Me, when ye shall search for me with all your heart."** Jer. 29:13 this will be accomplished only with devoted study and sincere prayer! So get out there with much prayer and study and find that needle! The Truth!

Jesus lets us know in His word that He is coming back for a single specific church, not a thousand! **"That He might present it to Himself** *a* **glorious church, not having spot, or wrinkle, or any such thing; but that it should**

190

be holy and without blemish." Eph. 5:27 The emphasis here is on the singular "a" church. This is the church that **"Keep the commandments of God and have the testimony of Jesus."** Rev. 12:17 and 14:12

Remember, the wheat and tares will grow together, and He will do the weeding at His soon second coming. So as to not be confused, God has given these two identifying characteristics of the people of His church in these last days during the final preparation of His return. Further examination of what these two characteristics are can be revealed biblically. **"And the dragon was wroth with the woman, and went to make war with the remnant of her seed, which keep the commandments of God, and have the testimony of Jesus Christ."** Rev. 12:17

Here, God is letting us know that the dragon (the devil) is wroth (angry) with the woman (the true church) and went to make war with them. Who are the "them" in this text? The people of God who have gone through great tribulation and have washed their robes and made their garments white in the blood of the LAMB! **"And one of the elders answered, saying unto me, 'What are these which are arrayed in white robes? And whence came they?' And I said unto him, 'Sir thou knowest.' And he said unto me, 'These are they which came out of great tribulation, and have washed their robes, and made them white in the blood of the Lamb.'"** Rev. 7:13 and 14

This is God's true church, folks! **"They that keep the commandments of God and have the testimony of Jesus Christ."** So God will come back for a people that will be a commandment-keeping people in their walk with Christ, and they will also have his testimony. And what is His testimony? **"For the testimony of Jesus is the Spirit of Prophecy."** Rev. 19:10 *"Here is the patience of the saints: here are they that keep the commandments of God, and the faith of Jesus."* Rev. 14:12

According to the word of God (Jesus Christ), this group will be few compared to the many that have had every opportunity to come to Him with a whole heart to take the straight and narrow way, but they chose to seek their own pathway instead. He said for us (the few) to find the straight and narrow way, **"Enter ye in at the strait gate; for wide is the gate, and broad is the way, that leadeth to destruction, and many there be which go in thereat: Because strait is the gate, and narrow is the way, which leadeth unto life, and few there be that find it."** Matt. 7:13 and 14

Again, many people are looking for designer religions! They want to do whatever is comfortable for them and not follow a straight thus saith the Lord! Jesus is only taking back with Him those who do the will of God and follow Him at His word. **"And why call ye Me, Lord, Lord, and do not the things which I say?"** Lk 6:46

There will be many in that day that perisheth because they refused to come out of their comfort zone and follow God at His word. But they who are faithful, holy, and just will He come back to get and to take part in His righteousness. For the word expressly declares, **"Blessed and holy is he that hath part in the first resurrection: on such the second death hath no power, but they shall be priests of God and of Christ, and shall reign with Him a thousand years."** Rev. 20:6

It is imperative that all of God's children be in that number because this is the true church of God. This church is made up exclusively by God and not by men. **"But ye believe not, because ye are not of My sheep, as I said unto you, 'My sheep hear My voice, and I know them, and they follow Me: And I give unto them eternal life; and they shall never perish, neither shall any man pluck them out of My Father's hand.'"** John 10:26–28 Until then, the jewels that makes up this church must live by faith and not by sight. **"For therein is the righteousness of God revealed from faith to faith: as it is written, 'The just shall live by faith.'"** Rom. 1:17

FAITH
THE SUBSTANCE OF THINGS HOPED FOR

Faith, according to the infallible word of God (Jesus Christ) because the word was made flesh, gives us the true definition of faith and how to exercise our faith. If God had not given us everything we needed to inherit eternal life and how we should live out our lives down here, then He would not have been the great God that He is. We would have been limited to our access to heaven. We would have had to try to find a way there for ourselves which is impossible to do. In every particular of life pertaining to this world and the world to come concerning the salvation of man, He has given for our admonition, welfare, and spiritual well-being, including but not limited to the very definition of faith He has given us. **"Now faith is the substance of things hoped for, the evidence of things not seen."** Heb. 11:1

God, through His infinite wisdom, gives every person at birth a certain measure of faith. How that measure of faith is cultivated, grown, and utilized is up to the individual. **"For I say, through the grace given unto me, to every man that is among you, not to think of himself more highly than he ought to think; but to think soberly, according as God hath dealth to every man a measure of faith."** Rom. 12:3

Each person's faith growth rate is directly proportional to the amount of exercise thereof. For example, if the right arm of a person is exercised frequently with a weighted barbell, it would not be long before that arm sees a noticeable strengthening and muscle growth in comparison to the left arm not being exercised by the person. Taking it a step further, let us say the left arm is tied to the body and not used for a considerable length of time. This left arm would become numb and unusable at some point in time. It would become atrophied, and if this process is continued, it would become totally useless. (Are there any who claim to be a member of God's true church that fit into this category?) The strength of this left arm would have to slowly be rebuilt before it could become of any good use, and so it is with the development of faith.

Again, God gives at birth every person a measure of faith. It is how that faith is exercised, used, or the lack of use that determines how it will grow or if it will become dwarfed and eventually vanish. If not used, it continues to approach the value of zero until it disappears altogether. If faith is used, on the other hand, it will continue to grow until that day of Christ's appearing. **"And Jesus said unto them, 'Because of your unbelief, for verily I say unto you, If you have faith as a grain of mustard seed; ye shall say unto this mountain, Remove hence to yonder place; and it shall remove; and nothing shall be impossible unto you. Howbeit this kind goes not out but by prayer and fasting'. "** Matt. 17:20 and 21

Little fasting is being done today, not to mention prayer! Fasting is a conscientious physical deprivation of food by not eating to obtain spiritual continuity with God. Spiritual things are spiritually discerned. To give an example, most parents, if they had a child who was hungry, they would do all in their power to feed that child. That is, if they love their baby. The Bible does not give detailed explanation or the scientific analysis as to what takes place when fasting. However, it does give the results to all who were seeking God's attention through faith. God as a loving Father would give His attention to His fasting child who is hungry and in most cases show His power because of the act of fasting and prayer. Even though there may be food available to the child of God, but when the child of God denies himself food for that spiritual connection with his Father in heaven, it somehow gets His attention better than with prayer alone. Read the prayer of Daniel in chapter 9 and notice how quickly God responded to Daniel's prayers and supplications after much fasting.

Take another look at this phenomenon called faith from a different perspective. Say for instance a person was born in the year of 1932 and lived to the present year of 2012. For simplicity's sake, let us say that they were born and died in the same month. That would put them exactly at a nice ripe old age of eighty years. When this hypothetical person was first born, it is a good chance the parents were very happy that a new baby was granted unto them. Newborns almost always bring joy with them. In most cases, the mother and the father would be the most joyful of the newborn entering into the world. However, in these turbulent times of today, it is not uncommon to find unwanted babies in garbage dumpsters. In many other pregnancies due to sexual lusts and lasciviousness, it would not be a big surprise if the attending medical personnel were not more joyful than the parents to see the new life enter into this world.

God told Adam and Eve to be fruitful and multiply. He later told Abraham the same thing. Married couples were to fill the earth with God-fearing children to build up His kingdom in heaven but due to selfishness, pleasure seeking, and a lack of resources, this world is teaching differently. The world is advocating having few children or none at all. This is in direct contradiction to the will of God. "And God blessed them, and God said, **'Be fruitful and multiply, and replenish the earth, and subdue it.'** Gen.1:28 The world is not following this practice; it is almost as available and common to get an abortion as it is to get a manicure these days. People want the satisfaction achieved by satisfying their sexual lusts but not the responsibility of raising a God-fearing child.

There are terrible troublesome times ahead, and at these times it is that people will be dismayed to see offspring come into the world. And because of sinful, pleasure-loving, flesh-satisfying desires, abortion rates are already off the charts **"But woe to them that are with child, and to them that give suck in those days!"** Mk 13:17 **"For, behold, the days are coming, in the which they shall say, Blessed are the barren, and the wombs that never bare, and the paps which never gave suck."** Lk 23:29

In most cases though, someone is around that is happy to see the new birth. Be it doctors, nurses, or the parent, someone is happy. This birth took place in 1932. Eighty years later in the year 2012, the same month this person was born, he passed away. Now someone is very sad and unhappy that their loved one is gone. Imagine now he is lying in his casket with his final nice-looking "go to church" clothes on. Depending on how this person lived his life, there may be some even happier to see him gone and dead in his coffin than those who rejoiced at his birth. But in most cases, there will be loved ones who are very heart broken and sad that this person is now departed. They have lived eighty long years. Now let us, at this point, examine some of their accomplishments and some of their life's endeavors.

They grew up in a relatively fashionable home and may or may not have gone to one of the fashionable churches of their day. They played childish games and wanted the fashionable toys of the times. They wanted the fashionable clothing and fashionable electronic equipment that most children want at a young age. More than likely, they wanted to go to the fashionable parties and attend the fashionable events that young people wanted to attend in their day. As they grew older, now they want the fashionable car and go to the fashionable universities as the other young adults were driving and going to. Now they are going to the fashionable parties and attending the fashionable events that young adults go to at the universities. They may or may not have joined a fashionable fraternity/sorority that most fashionable students join. They may or may not have attended a fashionable church that the majority of fashionable people attended. They made pretty good grades at the fashionable university. Now they seek the fashionable job that will pay a lot of fashionable money so that they can lead a fashionable lifestyle and take fashionable vacations. Hopefully, they marry the love of their life. Maybe it was that person who fashionably caught their eye as a young person. (Is it any wonder why the divorce rate is so high in this country?) They fashionably have children, and the process regurgitates itself all over again. While the world follows the pattern of this hypothetical person, is it any wonder why the world is in the condition it's in? *(it sin)*

However, because we are made of dust and with the passage of time, the processes becomes more and more degenerate. Due to multimedia devices and the way of the world, children today will experience instances of immorality at an earlier age than children did in preceding years. With the passage of time and with every succeeding generation, it appears that on a whole, beginning with the children, people become less respecting of themselves, parents, and authoritative figures. **"This know also, that in the last days perilous times shall come. For men shall be lovers of their own selves, covetous, boasters, proud, blasphemers, disobedient to parents, unthankful, unholy. Without natural affection, trucebreakers, false accusers, incontinent, fierce, despisers of those that are good; Traitors, heady, highminded, lovers of pleasures more than lovers of God."** 2 Tim. 3:1–5

Because in most cases, children are raised with the same fashionable desires that their parents were raised up with. But as time goes on, people grow to have an increased ability to obtain materialistic gains; children develop wanting more at a younger age and on a larger scale. This is why it is so gravely important to raise your children up in the love and admonition of the LORD and out in the country if possible! **"And, ye fathers, provoke not your children to wrath, but bring them up in the nurture and admonition of the Lord."** Eph. 6:4 **"And these words, which I command thee this day, shall be in thine heart; And thou shalt teach them diligently unto thy children, and shalt talk of them when thou sittest in thine house, and when thou walkest by the way, and when thou liest down, and when thou risest up."** Deut. 6:6 and 7

Now our person lies fashionable in their pretty clothes, while in their fashionable casket with many fashionable flowers that cost a lot of fashionable money. Only to be covered up with the same thing that they were made from, *unfashionable dirt!* Even you yourself will return to unfashionable dust. **"In the sweat of thy face shalt thou eat bread, till thou return unto the ground; for out of it wast thou taken: For dust thou art, and unto dust shalt thou return."** Gen. 3:19 ALL IS VANITY!

Sure, most people have a considerable amount of noteworthy accomplishments in their lifetime. They may have taken care of their families, raised their children, paid their bills, etc. But if a wholehearted assessment takes place and it is considered from a spiritual perspective, those accomplishments do not amount to a hill of red beans if the accomplishments did not include JESUS! **"For what shall it profit a man, if he shall gain the whole world, and lose his own soul? Or what will a man give in exchange for his soul?"** Matt. 12:26

Youth in this day and age waste a lot of precious time to a tremendous amount of dream chasing, attempting to build those proverbial castles in the sand. Then when they hit those silver and golden years of their lives, they begin to settle down somewhat but still chasing in a calmer less aggressive way, that very unlikely pie in the sky. It can be hoped at this point that they are not weighed in the balances by God and found wanting. (As did Belshazzar, king of Babylon at the time when he saw the "handwriting on the wall.")

The eighty short years of life has gone by like dust in the wind. Only for what seems like a moment are we here in comparison to the larger scheme of things and the age of time. **"Lord, make me to know mine end, and the measure of my days, what it is that I may know how frail I am. Behold, Thou hast made my days as an handbreadth, and mine age is as nothing before Thee; verily every man at his best state is altogether vanity. Selah. Surely every man walks in a vain show; surely they are disquieted in vain; he heap up riches, and knows not who shall gather them."** Ps. 39:4–6

All truly indeed is vanity. Even if eighty short years of life were lived to the fullest and attained many of the material tangibles that most of the world seek after, except for the clothes on your back, you go down to the grave with pretty much the same as you came into this world with. Absolutely nothing materialistically! There is, however, an unseen heavenly record that keeps a "down to the minute" accurate account of not so much of your physical accomplishments but of your moral and spiritual deeds. **"And I saw the dead, small and great, stand before God; and the books were opened and another book was opened, which is the book of life: and the dead were judged out of those things which were written in the books, according to their works."** Rev. 20:12

The only thing that goes into the grave with you is your character and the works thereof. And it is only the faith in and the Christ like character you displayed down here that will ultimately get you up at the last day.

Unlike faith, the fundamentals of science are primarily based on the parameters of what you can see, touch, taste, smell, and hear. In other words, science deals basically with the five anatomical senses of the human body. Of these five anatomical senses, most scientifically derived premises are established or rejected. Somewhere somebody determined that science could only be proven through the anatomical senses of man. That's kind of scary if you really think about it. The parts that deal with the rest of human nature—spirituality, faith, love, and the such—science seems to ignore or is very negligible in its recognition of these aspects of you and those that concern your faith. For example, how you love, who you love, the depth of your love, who/what you believe in, how and who you worship. The list could go on and on. There is no measuring rod to declare the depth of your love or the extent of your faith. Science cannot touch these aspects of your being, and they are that part of you that really defines you and what kind of person you are, not only the physical parts of you that can be seen, touched, or heard of you. A person can be dressed in the finest attire, smell of the most lustful fragrances, and speak with the smoothest sophisticated speech and be the biggest fake or devil that you could ever meet! As a matter of experiences, this is most often the case in this world.

We inherently cater to and are attracted by the flamboyant and charismatic. Jesus gives us a good example in the book of James and is a good tool for self-examination. **"For if there come unto your assembly a man with a gold ring, in goodly apparel, and there come in also a poor man in vile raiment** [*clothing*]**; And you have respect to him that wears the gay clothing, and say unto him, 'Sit here in a good place', and say to the poor, 'Stand there, or sit here under my footstool.' Are you not then partial in yourselves, and are become judges of evil thoughts?"** James 2:2–4

In other words, a person can look good, smell good, and talk good and not be good for you! (Spiritual things are spiritually discerned.) God is more interested in the spiritual man, not the physical man. **"But the Lord said unto Samuel, 'Look not on his countenance, or on the height of his stature, because I have refused him. For the Lord sees not as man sees, for man looks on the outward appearance but the Lord looks on the heart.'"** 1 Sam. 16:7

However, this is not how the world teaches. The world teaches from the youth up the side of the scientific. That is, to focus on the physical. How well your body is in shape, how attractive you look, how sweet you smell, and your ability to orate. These things should not be neglected, but when we nurture the spiritual man, the physical will always fall into place, and if we teach these values or principles to our children, the world may be a better place. **"But let it be the hidden man of the heart, in that which is not corruptible, even the ornament of a meek and quiet spirit, which is in the sight of God of a great price."** 1 Pet. 3:4

If we cater more to the physical man, then the spiritual man is neglected and becomes dwarfed. It is our duty to seek out and find the truth of God's word and as we do, our faith is enhanced. **"So then Faith cometh by hearing and hearing by the Word of God."** Rom. 10:17

Only sincere studying with faithful prayer will open up to the devoted a well of knowledge, understanding, and insurmountable joy! **"Study to shew thyself approved unto God, a workman that needeth not to be ashamed, righty dividing the Word of Truth."** 2 Tim. 2:15

While touching on spiritual things, if Adam and Eve had not fallen to sin, science of a higher order based on the spiritual very well may have been the focus of our study in this life. But because of sin and the degradation thereof, the study of science as we know it, is again, based on the human physical anatomical senses. That is, of the lower order, the physical and not the spiritual man. However, if sin had not entered into the world that a spiritual God has made, our deepest studies may very well have been devoted to the spiritual and those elements of life that only faith can accomplish. That is the higher order of our being—the spiritual. Such as, without lifting a finger by faith, moving the proverbial mountain (that happens to be literal) that Jesus spoke of; or the walking on water that Peter was able to mimic Jesus for a short while until his faith wavered, causing him to doubt and he began to sink; or causing non-floatable objects to swim as Elisha did with the ax that swam back up to the top of the water to be retrieved by the man who lost it; or to snap your fingers and be in another location as Phillip had done after baptizing the Ethiopian eunuch; or to be able to walk through fire without fireproof clothing and not be burned as did Shadrach, Meshach, and Abednego when they were cast into a fiery furnace for going against popular laws concerning bowing down to a golden image that King Nebuchadnezzar had set up. And not to mention the dry bones the prophet Ezekiel prophesied to the four winds to give breath by God in the valley of dry bones. These are just a few of the scientifically unexplained phenomena that are mentioned in scripture that probably would have been the subject of our study, that is, if sin had not diminished the seeking of the spiritual and promoted the satisfying of the physical man.

Only by faith could we faithfully learn the spiritual, and it would all be accomplished through our faith in the Most Faithful, Jesus Christ our Lord.

These and similar spiritual sciences along with the amazing love, mercy, and grace of God will undoubtedly be the subject for the study of the redeemed throughout the ceaseless ages of eternity while glorifying God in the highest! Remember, **"Faith is the substance of things hoped for the evidence of things not seen."** Heb. 11:1

[Consider the diagram below of Brother Lee's Faith vs. Time Growth Curve.]

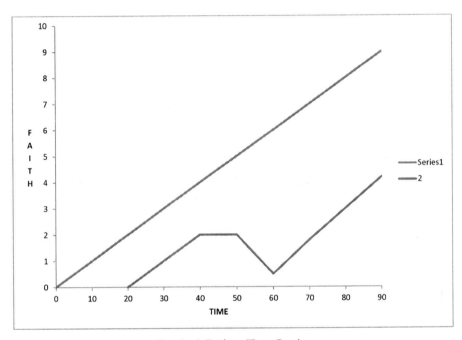

Bro. Lee's Faith vs. Time Graph:
Series Line 1 (blue line) represents the ideal faith curve which would be indicative of the faith of Jesus. Line 2 (the red line) is a graphical representation of the faith curve of a hypothetical person as he/she lives out their life.

This diagram is a graphical representation of a hypothetical person's faith as they traverse through life. The blue line or line 1 depicts the ideal growth of faith from birth. Notice how over time from birth the ideal faith curve, faith growth is directly proportional to time it never wavers but grows steadily upward and to the right. The only one who walked the earth where this ideal faith growth curve may be applied to is Jesus. Jesus is our example and the one whereby we must reference our lives. Even our faith should parallel Jesus' faith. **"For even hereunto were ye called: because Christ also suffered for us, leaving us an example, that ye should follow His steps."** 1 Pet. 2:21 Also consider these texts and make application of them. **"But the scripture hath concluded all under sin, which the promise by faith of Jesus Christ might be given to them that, believe."** Gal. 3:22 and **"Here is the patience of the saints: here are they that keep the commandments of God, and the faith of Jesus."** Rev. 14:12 In other words, if your faith growth curve does not reflect Jesus', though you may call yourself Christian, it is impossible to be one not walking in His faith reflecting Him. Because we are all sinners and have not always followed Christ, our faith growth curve can never be ideal from birth but at some point in our Christian walk, our faith should parallel that of Jesus' if we intend to live with Him throughout the ceaseless ages of eternity.

Let us consider this further by taking a look at line 2, the red line. This line is a graphical representation of a hypothetical person (it can be applied to any person's life). This person came to know Jesus at an early age of twenty years old. The curve shows this person coming to God by faith and continues walking and living by this faith. Notice with the passage of time how their personal spiritual or faith growth rate follows the exact path of the ideal faith growth curve as long as they hold on to JESUS. That is upward and to the right! In other words, only by their continued faith in Jesus and following Him at His word will parallel His faith in Him. **"Here is the patience of the saints: here are they that keep the commandments of God, and the faith of Jesus."** Rev. 14:12 Notice as you place your entire trust in God, the growth of your faith is directly proportional with time. Facing trials and hardships with prayer and fasting day by day, you become stronger and stronger in the Lord! **"Submit yourselves therefore to God. Resist the devil, and he will flee from you."** James 4:7

Our hypothetical person continues their walk experiencing the goodness of God and His blessings for about twenty years until about age forty. (Please keep in mind that this faith experience can be in range from any minimum to any maximum amount of time. A person can begin to backslide the same day that one gave his/her life to Christ as described by Him in the parable of seed sown on stony ground, but for simplicity's sake, a nice round figure of twenty years is applied for illustrational purposes.) As the graph illustrates, this person becomes proud and begin to trust in their own righteousness. **"Pride goeth before destruction, and a haughty spirit before a fall."** Prov. 16:18 **"When I shall say to the righteous, that he shall surely live; if he trust to his own righteousness, and commit iniquity, all of his righteousness shall not be remembered; but for his iniquity that he hath committed, he shall die for it."** Ezek. 33:13

Notice on the graph their spirituality begins to wane. They have begun to become less dependent upon God in their Christian walk. They have, in essence, reached a plateau. Without realizing it, our person has become a pew-bound Christian, and there is an explainable reason for this spiritual stagnation. They have lost the Holy Spirit's fire that once enlightened their countenance. Their personal devotion time with God has decreased. This person has little to no study and prayer time. They come to church, sit on the pew, and are spoon-fed by someone! Their faith is in jeopardy, and if not corrected will inevitably go negative.

Again this period of time, as with any other on the graph, can be very short or very long depending on the person and their level of strength, devotion, and commitment to God. A person can maintain any faith plateau for long periods of time and not be aware of it. In other words, they can become stagnated on any level.

There are people who have been in church for very long periods of time who are no better off now as to when they have begun to plateau. These people often can do the most damage to church growth and well-being as a whole because their influences have been felt for a long time. They often sit on church boards and can wreak havoc with their tongues by possibly having good orating skills and showmanship without the Spirit of God!

However, this hypothetical person has been given a ten-year plateau before as can be seen in the diagram; at age fifty, their faith begins to go negative, and they are now in a backsliding state of being. Their negative decline is directly proportional to their turning from God. Depending on whether or not the turning away from God is intentional or an unconscious gradual falling away determines the steepness of the downward curve. In other words, if this person at age fifty throws in the towel and says, "I'm done with this Christian stuff," gives up on God, and surrenders his faith, then the line at fifty years would shoot straight down on a negative decline, never to resurface unless a reconnection with Jesus is made. If they never turn back and regain their Christian faith, they too will shoot straight down to hell in the last day because they gave up on God. On the other hand, if he has an unconscious gradual decline from God, he is still going negative but not as rapidly. With this type of decline, it happens over an extended period of time as opposed to an instantaneous straight-down decline.

Actually, the persons who have platooned and are on the gradual decline may be worse off in getting it right with God than the persons who do not know Him. These persons are in a highly unfavorable lukewarm position with God. It is more difficult to show these people their errors than those who are cold. They have, in essence to some degree, hardened their hearts. You can't tell them anything! The people whose faith is paralleled with Jesus are good and need to make certain with prayer that they stay connected to and continue on with Him. **"I know thy works, that thou art neither cold nor hot: I would thou wert cold or hot. So then because thou art lukewarm, and neither cold nor hot, I will spue thee out of My mouth."** Rev. 3:15 and 16 The text is self-explanatory. Those who are lukewarm Christians, beware that Jesus says that He will spit you out.

They, along with other members of the church, may not even be aware of their condition and their deceptive negative influences in the church. Depending on their position and amount of influence with church functions, these church members' deceptions will start out imperceptible at first until they escalate to following man, and the entire church can be steered off course by these persons' suggestions and influences. **"For Israel slideth back as a backsliding heifer . . ."** Hos. 4:16 Notice the text is not talking about one man such as Jacob but the entire nation of Israel. The same scenario can be placed on not only an individual or an entire congregation but an entire religious organization.

Again there are some who continue going to church from week to week in this fallen condition and are unaware that Jesus saves us *from* our sins, not *in* our sins. They may not have much influence on the church's direction but believe they will be saved just by coming to church from week to week without holistically giving their lives to the only one who can save. God admonishes to turn again unto Him. **"Return, ye backsliding children, and I will heal your backslidings. Behold, we come unto thee; for thou art the LORD our GOD."** Jer. 3:22

Going back to the faith chart, this hypothetical person continues on a downward spiral for about ten years, then they begin to recognize their backsliding and at approximately age sixty come to a realization that they have not been following Jesus and sinking rapidly up to their nostrils in sin. With deep confession, prayer, and with a whole heart, pleads for forgiveness and are ready to turn back to Him. Immediately, the downward decline comes to a screeching halt and the curve begins to go positive that is upward and to the right with the passage of time. This person's faith over time, as illustrated in the diagram, begins to parallel Jesus' faith again, and if they continue in His faith, they will surely go home with Him at the end of time. Praise be to God!

Please note that more often than not, this kind of repentance usually does not happen automatically. There is often some type of outside intervention that takes place to bring a person to this kind of repentant realization that would bring about a dramatic change in one's life altering the course of their salvation. Often it is associated with some hardship or calamity that takes place in the life. Hardly ever does one concludes and simply turn to the Lord for turning's sake and say, "It's me, it's me, it's me O' Lord standing in the need of prayer," without some external influence acting on them. It takes an *external* event to get the backsliding soul's attention, slow them down, and cause them to have an *internal* look and think more about their *eternal* salvation.

Problems, such as an illness, death, financial troubles, relationship problems, you know things of this world that will quickly get your undivided attention. Whatever the deceptive vice Satan may use against you to cause the initial backsliding from Jesus, with a sincere heart, Jesus can make it all right again! **"If we confess our sins, He is faithful and just to forgive us our sins, and to cleanse us from all unrighteousness."** 1 John 1:9

If an external event is imposed upon the person in this illustration and their attention is not redirected to the good paths of righteousness, then as the graph indicates they would continue on a downward spiral straight to hell. But as can be seen and with good news, the trial in their life had its desired effect. The person reversed his ways, repented, confessed and gave a full surrender to Jesus, and at sixty years of age heading upward and to the right straight into heaven. Christ, along with all the holy angels, would welcome our hypothetical person there with open arms. **"Blessed are they that do His commandments that they may have a right to the tree of life, and may enter in through the gates into the city."** Rev. 22:14

Of course, the ideal situation would be for one to walk perfectly with God their entire lives as did Noah, Daniel, and Job to name a few. They excelled in living a Godly life holding on to their faith continually growing upward and to the right their entire lives. However, in today's world, this is hardly the case! Exceptional cases, such as Noah, Daniel, and Job are where every professed follower of Christ should want to be. **"Though Noah, Daniel, and Job were in it, as I live, saith the Lord GOD, they shall deliver neither son nor daughter; they shall but deliver their own souls by their righteousness."** Ezek. 14:20

Most people in these times experience a life of faith with ups and downs more realistic to the one depicted on the graphical illustration. Based on every individual's spiritual strengths, weaknesses, desires, commitments, abilities, etc., determines the length of the curve from any one point to another. **"Hearken; Behold, there went out a sower to sow: And it came to pass, as he sowed, some fell by the way side, and the fowls of the air came and devoured them up. And some fell on stony ground, where it had not much earth; and immediately it sprang up, because it had no depth of earth: But when the sun was up, it was scorched; and because it had no root, it withered away. And some fell on among thorns, and the thorns grew up, and choked it, and it yielded no fruit. And other fell on good ground, and did yield fruit that sprang up and increased; and brought forth, some thirty, and some sixty, and some an hundred. And He said unto them, 'He that hath ears to hear, let him hear.'"** Mark 4:3–9

How your personal faith curve is etched out is directly proportional to the choices you make on a daily basis for the rest of your life. Therefore, determine in your heart that this day forward, you will, day by day, live by faith growing daily upward and to the right in Christ Jesus. Amen. **"For therein is the righteousness of God revealed from faith to faith: as it is written, 'the just shall live by faith.'"** Rom. 1:17

CONCLUSION

When a defective short is in a power cord, it will prevent any electrical apparatus from operating as it should. So it is with this earth marred by sin. Sin can be viewed as a spiritual defective spot within the spiritual circuitry of this earth. As the defect in an electrical power cord needs to be removed and the original spliced back for uninterrupted continuity and smooth electrical flow, so does the defects of sin and its effect on this earth also needs to be removed for streams of righteousness and holiness to flow.

Once the spot of sin (represented by the oval) is forever removed from the universe, as can be seen in the above illustration, the sweet line of continuity and communion with Christ will forever return back to its glorious state as was intended by GOD in the first place. **"Seeing then that all these things shall be dissolved, what manner of persons ought ye to be in all holy conversation and godliness. Looking for and hasting unto the coming of the day of God, wherein the heavens being on fire shall be dissolved, and the elements shall melt with fervent heat? Nevertheless we, according**

to His promise, look for new heavens and a new earth, wherein dwelleth righteousness. Wherefore, beloved, seeing that ye look for such things, be diligent that ye may be found of Him in peace, without spot, and blameless." 2 Pet. 3:11–14

Let's face it, the day is far spent and along with this book, this world is rapidly reaching its conclusion. "Lift up your eyes to the heavens, and look upon the earth beneath: for the heavens shall vanish away like smoke, and the earth shall wax old like a garment, and they that dwell therein shall die in like manner: but My salvation shall be forever, and My righteousness shall not be abolished." Isa. 51:6

That is right; this old test tube we call Earth is wearing out! It's time for the new! Since there was a beginning to all of this, there has got to be an end of all this. "And I saw a new heaven and a new earth: for the first heaven and the first earth were passed away; and there was no more sea." Rev. 21:1

Jesus is coming back for those who have shown themselves worthy because the testing that has taken place in every life for the purpose of eternal salvation was not a man-made test! It is not about a man-made designer religion! Only those who have taken on the realistic righteousness of Christ are going home with Him when He comes. Remember, my friend, He is coming back for a church without spot or wrinkle! There are no smoke screens or hocus pocus; only the righteous will enter in! Remember, it is about following God at His Word wherever you may be. Please do not get caught up in and priding yourself with the formalities of church gathering from week to week and following man. With diligent prayer and studying of God's word, there should be one and only one alternative. One pathway! One way in Christ! One faith! It is the solemn duty of the reader with much prayer to find this faith and this path and get on it and stay on it! Don't ever forget, "One Lord, one faith, one baptism" Eph. 4:5 and look for God while there is still time. "Seek ye the LORD while He may be found, call ye upon Him while He is near." Isa. 55:6

AUTHOR'S PAGE

Born down in the deep south of Mississippi, the parents of author L. E. Lee moved north to Chicago with him as an infant in arms at the age of seven months old. It was here where he grew up and spent the first years of his life on the challenging south side of the Windy City at the Robert Taylor housing projects. Those early years there in Chicago is where, at the tender age of seven years, he came to know God.

While in the second grade at Coleman Elementary School, an incident happened that Lee was blamed for but something that he did not do. Having a feeling of being trapped in deep trouble and the thought of getting a thrashing from his dad for something he did not do overwhelmed him, and at that tender age of seven, he began to pray. While privately in his bedroom and on his knees, Lee made three separate requests of God and much to his relief, all of which were granted to him that selfsame day. This petitioning to God in prayer and God answering is what deepened the impression of God in his heart for later trials and pitfalls he would encounter on life's journeys.

After overcoming many challenges, Lee at the age of twenty while at the University of Kentucky, had a very close, personal, and intimate relationship with God. He is convinced that during this time in his life, God showed him things that He normally does not show everyone. One night while asleep alone in his room, the room began to shake and a deep darkness, one that could be felt, overshadowed the room. While considering this darkness, in his trance, Lee saw a bright light as the sun shines in its strength. The light did not pass into the darkness neither did the darkness creep into the light, but there was a distinct division between the two, and a voice came out of the light which commanded, **"Leave him alone! Let him decide. Let him make the choice."** Lee believes the voice that came out of the light in this vision was none other than Jesus Christ Himself who prevented the deep dark presence, whom he believes to have represented Satan, from taking him without a cause. This internal battle the forces of light vs. darkness have been raging ever since, but L.E. Lee has long since decided to give his entire life to the God of Heaven.

Fifteen years ago, L.E. Lee was inspired to write *Living in a Test Tube*. However, because of his experience with many people appearing to have a form of godliness and not attempting to holistically follow God at His Word; as Jonah thought his preaching to the peoples of Nineveh would be of no avail, Lee also lack the belief that his writings would accomplish their desired intent for the promotion of good and righteousness therefore he left off from completing the book until recently. Also because of his scientific background, he graphically draws upon scientific parallels to biblical references, reflecting the inspirational views of how life here on earth is primarily a test, how the planet earth is the test tube environment, how earth would be a much better place if God's way was followed, and what it is that the great God of heaven has in store for those who love and serve Him.

It is the hope and prayer of the author that every person who reads this book will at least engage in deeper spiritual reflection and at most turn with a sincere heart to prepare for what is to come upon this "test tube" called planet Earth.